SURF CITY

SURF CITY
THE JAN & DEAN STORY

DEAN TORRENCE

SelectBooks, Inc.
New York

This edition published by SelectBooks, Inc.
For information address SelectBooks, Inc., New York, New York.

First Edition

ISBN 978-1-59079-395-4

Library of Congress Cataloging-in-Publication Data

Names: Torrence, Dean, 1940-
Title: Surf city : the Jan & Dean story / Dean O. Torrence.
Description: First edition. | New York : SelectBooks, [2016] | Includes bibliographical references and index.
Identifiers: LCCN 2016023049 | ISBN 9781590793954 (pbk. : alk. paper)
Subjects: LCSH: Torrence, Dean, 1940- | Berry, Jan, 1941-2004. | Jan and Dean. | Singers--United States--Biography.
Classification: LCC ML420.T705 A3 2016 | DDC 782.42166092/2 [B] --dc23
LC record available at https://lccn.loc.gov/2016023049

Book cover design by Dean O. Torrence
Book interior design by Janice Benight

Manufactured in the United States of America
10 9 8 7 6 5 4 3 2 1

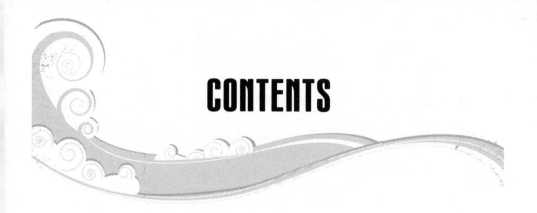

CONTENTS

FOREWORD

Jan & Dean, believe it or not, had a hand in the origins of The Beach Boys. When we heard them on the radio in the late fifties and early sixties, it encouraged my cousins and me to record "Surfin'" because we figured if they had made it, anybody could make it. Even the Bomp Bomp Dip Ta Dip Ta Dips were similar to what we heard from the Uni High School Duo.

Over the years, we have had so much fun, fun, fun and so many memorable interactions. Whether it was onstage in Hawaii at the KPOI Million Dollar Party in July 1964, or on the *T.A.M.I. Show* in October 1964 that Jan & Dean hosted, we enjoyed a healthy rivalry as well as friendship.

Whether it was coming up with The Beach Boys logo and the *15 Big Ones* album cover, or the tremendously popular art for the 50 Years of "Fun, Fun, Fun" tour and the 50 Years of "Good Vibrations" tour merchandise featuring the VW bus with the peace symbol, Dean has been an ongoing creative presence in our life. His Grammy-nominated and award-winning Kittyhawk Graphics work is an important part of his resume, and The Beach Boys have been the beneficiary of his creative efforts.

Dean and I have done some memorable things together over the years, whether it was Spring Break concerts for Budweiser as Mike and Dean or recording Christmas songs together. I was also invited by Dean to do a cameo appearance for the movie *Deadman's Curve*. Plus, one of our biggest hits featured my cousin

Brian and Dean on the high falsetto part in "Barbara Ann" featured on *The Beach Boys' Party!* album. You should check out the 50th anniversary edition of the *Party!* album that features all three versions of the recording of "Barbara Ann," pretty funny stuff!

To this day, whenever the occasion permits, Dean will join us on stage. It's always like a reunion—good friends having a great time together. I'm certain you, the reader, will have a great time reading this story that Dean shares with us of his life experience, his Surf City Saga.

Peace and Love,
Mike Love

1

THE FOUR-CAR
GARAGE BAND

{1957–1958}

itting in a stuffy classroom in the mid-1950s wishing lunch was less—a lot less—than an hour away. Wishing that three o'clock were sooner—a lot sooner. Wishing June 17, the last day of classes before summer vacation, was tomorrow. My mind was really drifting, even more than usual. I looked longingly out the window on this typically beautiful spring day in West Los Angeles. The sprinklers were running. It was a beautiful sound because it meant that summer was just around the corner. The damp grass smelled wonderful! I was daydreaming about what a great weekend was coming up . . . and the one after that . . . and the one after that. Okay, I thought, all weekends past and future were the greatest! But then it occurred to me that the only thing better than a weekend was summer vacation. Now, that was really the greatest!

Whoa! All of a sudden I spot something very much out of the normal range of things to be viewed from this window. There is a student walking outside of the school grounds, on the other side of the fence, mind you, a place that 99.9 percent of the student body would never even consider being. Remember, this was the fifties.

Now, not only is this guy not in class, strolling down the street on the other side of the fence, walking in plain view of the many class-rooms facing the street for everybody to see, including teachers, but this guy is smoking a cigar! What fuckin' nerve! What an asshole, I thought. Hey, isn't that Jan Berry, the rich kid from Bel Air? This guy is blond, good-looking, he is wearing a gray club jacket, he is swaggering, he's on the other side of the fence, and he is puffing on a big stogie. Yep, that's got to be Jan Berry. What an arrogant asshole!

That was my first recollection of William Jan Berry, one of the smartest kids in school, one of the best looking guys in school, and an exceptional athlete to boot. Did I leave out anything? Oh, yeah. He came from one of the wealthiest families in West Los Angeles.

Well, my geometry class did finally end and three or four weeks later summer did eventually arrive and we did get to do what most of our teenage friends did—hit the beach. The beach during summer vacation was the center of our universe. My typi-cal summer vacation day started off by sleeping in. Then there would be breakfast outdoors on the patio, sharing buttered cinna-mon toast with my favorite blue jay, Mr. Blue. Then it was time to load up my truck with all my beach gear. In the bed of the truck, under a tarp, I kept a twelve-foot balsa wood surfboard, a pair of black pin-striped water skis I had made myself in wood shop, two sets of fins for body surfing, two volleyballs and socks (just in case the sand was too hot), a football, a gym bag full of towels, extra bathing suits, a tube of Coppertone, a deck of cards, and one of the most important beach items—a portable radio with the dial preset to KFWB, "Color Radio." The drive from my house in West Los Angeles to the beach was as important to the overall experience as the day at the beach itself.

Slipping behind the wheel of the '32 Ford Deuce pickup truck with over thirty coats of white lacquer, I was now smelling the scent of new tuck-and-roll leather seats blended with the sweet smells of Coppertone suntan lotion and transmission grease. This was indeed paradise. All of my senses were being bombarded as the sunshine bounced off of the chrome goodies. My unique four-exhaust pipe system, which I had designed myself, made a very distinctive sound. I would pop open a cold bottle of Dr. Pepper, hold it between my legs, switch on the radio tuned to my favorite top 40 station, and off I'd go.

My favorite radio station was KFWB Color Radio. They played our music, young people's music. Teenagers finally had their own music. My parents were still listening to Perry Como, Dean Martin, and Doris Day. The college kids were listening to the Kingston Trio, Harry Belafonte, or Peter, Paul and Mary. We were listening to the Del-Vikings, Dion and the Belmonts, Frankie Avalon, Fats Domino, Carl Perkins, The Platters, Little Richard, The Cadillacs, The Five Satins, The Diamonds, The Everly Brothers, Sam Cooke, Ricky Nelson, the Coasters, and Elvis.

The route to the beach rarely changed. North up Beverly Glen, through the beautiful Holmby Hills, then left on Sunset heading west. Just past the entrance to UCLA there was a sweeping right-hand curve we affectionately called "Dead Man's Curve." Next I would pass the gate to Bel Air and drive on through Brentwood, past Will Rogers State Park and on to Pacific Palisades. If I was going surfing I would continue west on Sunset until I hit Pacific Coast Highway (PCH), turning north heading to Malibu and eventually settling in at "The Pit." But most of the time I would turn left down a winding palm tree-lined road called Chautauqua, which would place me in Santa Monica Canyon. I loved catching my first glimpse of the Pacific Ocean.

Most of us were too cheap to pay for parking, so the process of looking for parking space was an integral part of the ritual. Once parked, even the walk to the beach was special. The sweet smell of the ocean wafting up the canyon was proof that you had arrived.

Approaching PCH on the way to the beach, the aroma of hamburgers and onions being grilled at Roy's filled the air. Mr. Novak would be standing outside his shop checking out all the girls in their bathing suits as they passed by his shop.

Next was the challenge of getting across PCH. There was a signal, but it was two blocks away. The cool guys would sprint straight across the street. The girls, nerds, and old folks would walk the two blocks to the signal or use the underpass. For me, the object was to get to the volleyball court as fast as possible because you had to sign up to play, and the wait was always at least an hour or more. So of course I sprinted across the street.

Once I signed up for volleyball it was time to go hang out with my beach buddies. We would gossip, listen to music, flirt, play cards, and wait for our big volleyball game. Having a good volleyball game was a really good way to impress the chicks. After a tough game, we were usually covered with sweat and sand, and the best remedy was to run as fast as you could straight into the 64-degree California surf. The feeling was exhilarating, and the water felt and tasted great. It would make you tingle all over. If the waves were exceptional, we'd do some body surfing. The sweet smell of the salt and the seaweed was so much a part of our summer days. What a great place to be in! What a great time to be a teenager! It just didn't get much better than this. We were all surely blessed!

Every summer my family would spend a month in a small rented house at 121 Agate Street on Balboa Island. Most of the kids there belonged to the Balboa Island Yacht Club, for a five dollar a year membership fee. There were days when we would get six small sailboats, or "Snow Birds," together and play sponge tag all day long. We would all meet at the Club's pier and draw straws to see who was "it." The rest of the players would all get in their sailboats and head off in different directions. The boat that was "it" would have to wait one minute before engaging in pursuit of any of the other sailboats. We would all head for different parts of the channel. The pursuing boat would try to chase down the closest or easiest boat to catch.

The strategy for the boat that was "it" was to get close enough to one of the other boats to be able to hit it with the wet sponge, but try to throw the sponge at a part of the boat (preferably the hull) where the sponge would ricochet off and fall into the water, giving the attacking boat time to turn around and get away. Or, the other strategy was to hit the target boat in the apex of the sail, the right-angle pocket where the boom and mast come together. Hitting the sail in this area with an extra wet sponge would cause the sail's sweet spot to get heavy with water, thus slowing down the new "it" boat.

This game would continue all day with pursuits covering miles around the three major islands, and in and out of the hundreds of pleasure crafts traveling the channel to and from the ocean. We had all packed lunches and brought soft drinks, so if we weren't involved in a major pursuit, we would eat or take a quick dip off the side of the boat. The game was over at a certain time. Whoever was "it" at that particular time would be the loser. We would all meet back at the Balboa Island Yacht Club's Beaks Pier, where we would hose down our boats, cover them up, and head off to the Jolly Roger Café for a hamburger and some ice cream—paid for, of course, by the loser.

Some mornings I would drive my truck off Balboa Island, going north on PCH, through Newport to the next beach community, Huntington Beach, driving past the pier until I reached Oil Rig Hill. After finding a parking place, I would slide my old, dinged balsa wood surfboard out of the back of my truck, climb down the ice plant embankment on to the warm sand, and head to the water.

Huntington Beach had great surf and lots of room for average surfers like me. Further north at Malibu Beach, where I first learned to surf, there was a much smaller beach where the better surfers monopolized the waves and would even, on occasion, intimidate beginning surfers or nonlocals (who we called hodads). Obviously, only the skillful local guys were having a good time chasing waves at Malibu Beach. But here at a Huntington Beach, there was a good seven miles of surf. Locals surfed by the pier, the best surfers would surf south of the pier, and the average surfers were north of the pier. I was usually way north of the pier.

Once I got my board to the water's edge, I would drop it down on the sand and then proceed to apply wax to the top of the surfboard. Wax repels the water off the top of the board, making it easier to stay on it once you are out in the water. Then it was time to paddle that big ol' long board out into the surf and try and catch some waves.

At night we would take the ferry across to the Fun Zone, which was kind of like a mini boardwalk. Or some nights, there might even be a rock 'n' roll concert at the Rendezvous Ballroom. I saw my very first rock 'n' roll concert there. All three acts had had hit records on the charts—Sunny Knight, Jesse Belvin, and Frankie Lymon and the Teenagers.

I remember being profoundly affected by watching Frankie Lymon and the Teenagers sing "Why Do Fools Fall in Love?" Until that time we, as rock 'n' roll enthusiasts, didn't know much about the artists we were listening to on the radio. There was hardly any rock 'n' roll on TV at the time, and not much in the print media either. Album covers were where we would get our first look at our rock 'n' roll heroes. They all looked a lot older to us than they were. We were sure they were as old as our parents. But Frankie Lymon was only fourteen, and the rest of his group were really teenagers. Wow! So were we! So, hey, maybe we could also make some music just like these guys! What do you think? Nnnnaaahhh!

In early September it was time to say good-bye to my Balboa Island pals and make a vow to see each other next summer. Back at home in LA, it was time to get ready for the football season. I was a wide receiver on our high school football team. At six foot one, I was 155 pounds, dressed of course, plus shoes, soaking wet, after dinner plus dessert.

For many years while growing up my dad would play quarterback and I would be the receiver. We would play on the front lawn of our quaint upper middle class, Spanish style home in West Los Angeles. My dad played football while he was at Stanford University, and it was hoped that I would follow in his cleat marks. We would play for hours upon hours. I'd run short routes, medium routes, streaks, button hooks, post patterns, corner routes, stop and goes, and I was always pleased when the inside of my biceps were black and blue because it meant I was catching a lot of balls in the right place. After catching the balls I would dodge and weave my way through shrubs and rosebushes to score a touchdown.

Our high school football team started meeting a couple of weeks before the start of fall semester. It was usually typical Southern California summer weather throughout the month of September. The sprinklers were sometimes still on when we arrived. The grass smelled sweet. It smelled like football. We would soak a towel in water and suck on it when we got thirsty. The scrimmages would last a couple of hours or until someone got hurt.

Then came the best part. The short walk, or bike ride, just down the street to the local Frosty Freeze, the West Coast equivalent to Dairy Queen. We were all so thirsty and for twenty cents you could buy a quart of Coke and plenty of soft ice cream. We would sit at the painted wooden tables and tell our summer stories, usually full of summer romances, usually greatly exaggerated. The girl was conveniently always from out of town, out of state, from New York, Chicago, Hawaii, Hong Kong, Pango Pango, or anywhere far enough away that the story couldn't be verified. But we hung on every single word. Teammates wouldn't lie to each other, would they?

Then it was the first day of school. New classes. New teachers. New classmates. New breasts. And at the end of the day, our new football equipment: pads, helmet, jersey, and a new sports locker to put them in. I looked around the room for my newly assigned locker. Finding it, I dialed the combination. My goodness, it works! I open the locker and it smells great, like some old sweaty shoulder pads. I sit on the bench in front of this bank of lockers and start to take off my shoes. I can't wait to get the pads on, and pull that jersey over those pads. Clank. Someone is opening the locker next to mine. I look up . . . oh, no! It's that rich kid, Jan Berry! He smokes cigars! He's too pretty! He doesn't even have a butch haircut. What's he doing here? He couldn't be going out for football, could he? He didn't work out with us, or scrimmage in those last hot days of summer. Does he think all he has to do is show up? Man, talk about an ego. Well, I won't talk to him. I'll pretend I don't even see him.

"Hi! I'm Jan." Oh, shit! I guess I have to say something to him now.

"Uh, hi. I'm Dean." Could I hear Humphrey Bogart saying, "This could be the start of a very interesting relationship"? Nah. This guy's an asshole. "Want some Milk Duds?" he asks me. Are you kidding me? I'm serious about football and I eat my last bit of food at "nutrition," the snack time in between my first class and lunch. So I eat all of my lunch at this time, around 10:15 a.m., and then at lunchtime I might have a banana and some liquid. By the time football practice rolls around at 3:30 p.m. I'm lean and mean.

"No thanks," I reply. God, what an asshole! How could he eat that crap just before a hard workout? This guy is obviously not an athlete. Wonder if next he'll be offering me a cigar!

"So Dean, what position do you play?" he asks.

"Uh, split end or flanker," I reply.

"Yeah, me too," he says. Oh, shit. That figures. "Hey, I've got to go take a dump," he tells me. Eating crap like that, no wonder he has to take a dump. "I'll see you out there," he says.

I finished getting on my uniform. I liked my new jersey and jersey number, 42. The jersey is royal blue, the piping and the number are orange with black trim. I lace up my black high-tops and head out of the locker room. The aluminum cleats made the neatest sound as we walked across the cement floor.

Once we were outside we had to cross over some asphalt, then the dirt track and finally on to what football was all about—grass! I couldn't wait to run on the grass. The feeling was such a high. The first couple of days we were doing mostly calisthenics and running. The weather was beautiful, warm with the usual ocean breezes keeping us cool. By the end of the week we were divided into our special groups: the offense on the east end of the field and the defense was on the west end. I was working out with the first team. The coach wanted me to play flanker. Jan Berry was working out as the split end. We were a couple of days away from our first game, so it was time to scrimmage against the defense.

Our offense was primarily a running attack. Quarterbacks in those days were not bred to be straight drop-back passers. They mostly handed off to multiple running backs or ran the ball themselves after faking it to someone. When they did pass it was usually some short route and usually over the middle, since that would be an easier pass for the quarterbacks to complete. On the running plays to my side, most of the time I would run deep patterns, taking the defensive back and safety with me down the field. On some runs to my side, I would get to blindside the defensive end or linebacker so the running back could get to the outside and run down the sidelines.

I wasn't very heavy as you may remember, but I was very quick and I liked contact, so a crackback block (a block coming from the outside in worked on even somebody a lot bigger than me) was no problem. On running plays to the opposite side, I would go down the field in search of someone to cream. The defensive backs were all about my size, and they would be trying to hunt down the ball carrier and not paying much attention to someone streaking down the field from the opposite side. Obviously, I didn't have many good friends in the defensive secondary.

Wow! They finally call a passing play! How rare! I was to run a curl in the seam between the linebacker and the defensive backs—right over the middle. I run the pattern. I'm behind the linebacker and in front of the defensive back and safety. I curl in toward the quarterback expecting the ball to be already on its way. No ball, but he's looking right at me. Oh, great! Everybody knows where it's going—especially my good friends the defensive backs that I have been blindsiding all day. I'm praying for the quarterback to get sacked. For God's sake, do not throw the ball to me now! Oh, shit! He does throw it to me, and it's a wounded duck pass, high and wobbling. The defensive backs were at full speed licking their chops, aiming right at my back. Two linebackers were on their way from the front and we all met in the middle. Crunch! They drove me backwards into the ground. I hit very hard on my tailbone, the coccyx. They all jumped up high fiving. I jumped up to show them I wasn't hurt. Seconds later I blacked out.

The next thing I remember I am sitting up drinking water. I'm told I can go take an early shower. The tip of my spine hurts a lot, but I didn't want anyone to know, so I sat for a while. Then, when no one was looking I headed for the locker room. I could barely walk. I really thought I had cracked my spine or something. That evening I went to my family doctor. Luckily he concluded that it was only a very badly bruised coccyx. The next day I attended practice, but I hurt way too much to play. They had to replace me, but I continued to work out, just with no contact. Jan Berry had made the team and was playing really well, of course!

Every day, as we got ready for football practice, Jan would offer me candy. Usually Milk Duds, but sometimes Red Hots. One day he spilled his box of Red Hots on the locker room floor. He was pissed. I wonder, will he get dressed, go to the school store, buy another box and then come back to practice? Shit, no! He is picking up each and every one of those Red Hots off the dirty floor where smelly athletes' feet have been, along with dirty jock straps, and once they are all back in the box he continues to eat them! What a fuckin' character. I almost laughed out loud. You know, I thought, maybe he's not such a bad guy.

"Got any Milk Duds left?" I asked.

"No. But I do happen to have some Red Hots!"

"Ahh, no thanks." He asked me what I was driving. Oh, yeah. He's seen my truck, he thinks it's really cool! "What do you drive?" I asked.

He was very proud of his '57 Chevy Bel Air, turquoise and white, fuel-injected 372 cubic inch. "Now that's extremely cool!"

After practice we would all hit the shower room. One afternoon someone was singing in the shower. It had such a great echo. The hit songs we were listening to in those days were your classic doo-wop songs. Lots of vocal parts, a lead voice, four or five-part harmonies, a bass voice part, and of course you had to have a falsetto part. Someone started to sing along with the original guy. Then Jan picked up a part and started singing. A couple of other guys chimed in. Hey, there is a part missing. Someone needs to sing the falsetto part, I thought. I looked around. Nobody took it, so I did.

I was working out with the team, but I wasn't playing because I was still injured and hadn't been cleared by my doctor to play. I soon realized that I was looking forward to the after practice shower room jam sessions more than I was football. And, we were even starting to sound good. That's relatively speaking of course. Our favorite song to sing was "Get a Job" by the Silhouettes. Another favorite was "Tell Me Why" by Norman Fox & The Rob-Roys. Others included "Short Shorts" by the Royal Teens and "I Wonder Why" by Dion and the Belmonts.

I kept working out with the team but I wasn't cleared to play contact until very late in the season. To be honest, my tailbone still hurt a lot, but I really wanted to play because as a senior it was my last year. As the football season drew to an end, our final play-off game on Saturday, November 29, 1957, against Banning High School, a perennial powerhouse, approached.

In the fourth quarter we were tied at fourteen all. We had the ball and I was on the bench. A third-down pass was thrown to my replacement, Paul Garcia, a really good athlete. It was another one of those floating balls that often gets a receiver hurt. Crunch! He was down hard. The ball rolled out of bounds, incomplete. Paul doesn't get up. A couple of trainers go out, pick him up, and drag him to the sidelines. It's fourth down and eight yards to go, deep in our own part of the field. Coach yells out, "Torrence, get in there!" So I got up, went out, and joined the huddle.

The quarterback calls for a flanker reverse. Oh, shit, that's me! I hadn't run that play in four months. It's fourth down! Doesn't he know that? We shouldn't be trying to run a play when it's fourth down, deep in our own territory, we need to punt the ball! But, should I run it anyway? Even if he doesn't know it's fourth down? I could be a big hero if I could make that first down and keep our drive alive...

"It's fourth down," I blurt out.

"Oh shit, yeah, better punt."

Relieved, I go out to my flanker position. I am on the left side-lines. Since I was one of the fastest guys on the team, it was my job to streak straight down the sidelines and to only cut in once the ball carrier committed to going up the middle.

I was in my three-point stance, looking down field. It was a dark and dreary late November afternoon. The fog had rolled in. It was damp and chilly—almost eerie. Standing all by himself at about the 10-yard line was Bannings senior, all-American Lynn Gaskill, who was committed to play college football at USC the following year. Boy, I think. I could make a name for myself if I could get quickly downfield and nail this guy. Maybe he will fumble. Maybe I can hit him and make him fumble. Maybe the ball will roll into the end zone and I can pounce on it. That would be six points! Maybe when he sees me bearing down on him he will let the ball go and I can down it inside the ten. Then we can hold them, make them punt, get great field position, and score with no time left on the clock! My mediocre season could all change in this one play!

The ball was snapped, and I took off like a shot. I was flying straight down the sidelines. Lynn is looking up through the mist for the ball. It should be reaching him any second. I am now getting close to him, so I cut in, even though he has not yet caught the ball. I am now five or six steps away from a collision. He is not calling for a fair catch.

Man, I am going to cream this all-American hot shot. Oh, shit, he is still looking up and I'm about to hit him and the ball has not arrived yet! A major penalty! Where the hell is the ball? I start to put on the breaks and just then he does catch the ball and puts a nifty little juke on me. I'm grabbing at his number 16 jersey and just getting air while he heads up the very same sidelines I was supposed to be protecting to score the winning touchdown. In that very moment, he was now totally committed to the next level of football while I was fully committed to finding something else.

I thought about how different things could have been if I had made that tackle. Why was I so concerned about taking that penalty that I had slowed down? Who's to say I couldn't have hit him just as the ball arrived and dropped him on the spot, or if I did end up just being a fraction of a second too early, big deal, it was a 15-yard penalty.

Our season was over. There was no singing in the shower after this game. Arriving back at our school after our long bus ride back from Banning, we turned in our equipment, our helmets and uniforms, then went to our lockers to clean them out and to turn in our locks. Jan was already cleaning out his locker by the time I arrived—mostly candy wrappers.

"Hey, Dean. Want an old Abba-Zaba? Or how about this 3 Musketeers bar?" Man, I couldn't believe it. I was depressed about the game, along with just about everyone else, and this guy was busy sorting out his candy reserves. "Hey, I'm having a party at my house tomorrow night. Here's my address and directions. It should be a great party. Lots of new 45s that nobody has heard yet, hope you can make it. Sure you don't want the Abba-Zaba?"

"No, thanks. But I will try to come to the party." Wow! Jan Berry's parties were legendary and I had just been invited to one. Normally Jan's parties were exclusively attended by the members of "The Barons," a YMCA sponsored club at our high school. The Barons were all a half semester behind me. My semester had its own clubs. So it was exciting to be welcomed into The Baron family. Well I have to be honest, the football loss was already starting to fade.

The next day I washed my truck, put a new coat of wax on it, and polished the chrome with special care given to the six chrome exhaust tailpipes. My truck was almost entirely white and everything that wasn't white was black or chrome. This also included everything in the engine compartment as well. One of my newest additions was an eight ball that I had borrowed from a local pool hall. I had drilled a hole in the eight ball and screwed it on to the end of my chrome gearshift lever. Why an eight ball? It's black and white! It looked really bitchin'.

Finally it was time to leave for the party. I put on my best jeans, my cleanest white t-shirt, and my University High School letterman's jacket. I took almost the same route I took to go to the beach, except right after Dead Man's Curve I turned right off of Sunset, through the Bel Air gates, and proceeded way up into the hills almost to the very top. Finding the address on the mailbox, 1111 Linda Flora Drive, I looked down the long driveway to a beautiful home out on a knoll overlooking the whole city below. It was breathtaking. I drove down the driveway to the parking area in front of the sprawling ranch house. There were lots of cool cars parked in the driveway—mostly Chevys and Fords. One was a fantastic looking grey Olds 88 with new spinner hubcaps. Jan's '57 Chevy was parked right next to a sailboat on a trailer. As I parked I noticed that I was the only one who had a truck. I took a deep breath and walked into the party.

The music was loud. People were dancing. Some guys were drinking. Some were even smoking. The girls were dressed to kill. Jan was on the dance floor. I waved hello. Over in the corner, next to the Ampex tape recorder that was playing all of the prerecorded music, were some of the guys from the team, and some other high school acquaintances—all singing along with the music. Nobody was singing the falsetto parts! I joined in. A few songs later Jan joins us with some of the other guys. It's sounding pretty good. Ever notice how good you think you sound when you sing along with a great record? Most of the dateless guys stuck around the tape recorder most of the evening. We had a blast.

Sometime during the festivities I noticed a man banging on one of the sliding glass windows. Nobody is paying any attention to him. I asked one of the guys, "Who is that man?" and he says, "Oh, that's Jan's Dad."

"Why is he outside trying to get in?" I wanted to know.

"Because he was taking some of the liquor away from the guys." Jan had this great idea. He told two guys to go out on the lawn and stage a fake fight. Then when Jan's dad went out to break up the fight, they ran back into the house and locked him out. Holy shit! This was inconceivable to me. Even my normally passive dad would have called the police or gotten into his car and driven it through a sliding glass window. The party would have been over—forever! But this guy is tapping on the window trying to get somebody's attention. Christ! When he gets back in the house our asses are gonna get kicked!

Soon thereafter the man disappears. Is he letting out all the air in our tires? Putting sand in our gas tanks? I asked someone if they knew where Jan's dad was. I was told that Jan had let his dad in and sent him to his room! The party went on until way after midnight. By the time all the guys with dates had departed, just the alleged singers were left, about eight to ten guys including Jan. I asked Jan where he got the tape with all the great music. "Follow me," he said.

He took me into a big playroom, which was once a four-car garage. Against one wall was a piano. Another wall had a counter-top with shelves. On the counter were two Ampex reel-to-reel tape recorders and a turntable. He also had a bunch of boxes filled with thousands of 45s filed in alphabetical order. He informed me that this was where he made the tape with all the music for the party, right there in his music room. I wondered how someone could have so many records and so many obscure ones at that. He took a piece of paper from the top of the piano and showed it to me. It had the logo of a radio station tower and lightning bolts with the call letters KJAN Radio and "The Voice of Bel Air" just below it. Typed on the letterhead is a letter to the promotion staff at a major record label asking for promotional records for the programming on KJAN Radio.

"You own a radio station, too?" I asked. He looked at me like I was a dumb ass.

"No, I don't own a radio station! But I do take print shop at school and Mr. Fugazawa let me print this letter up on my own sta-tionery, so I guess I do own the stationery. I mail this letter out to all of the record labels I can find an address for, and a few days later

I get at least five copies of each new release from every record company that I sent my letter to."

"Why five?" I wanted to know.

"Well, because KJAN Radio has five disc jockeys and each need their own record," he tells me. Then he adds, "You know, I probably average fifty to seventy-five records a day." What a brilliant scam! He then makes me one of his new disc jockeys on his radio station. "You have to be 'Dizzy Dean.'" Every disc jockey had to have a cool nickname. Jan's nickname was Jumpin' or Jivin' Jan. I can't recall the names of the other disc jockeys.

Jan goes on to tell me that he is thinking of forming a group to perform at an upcoming talent competition at our high school, and that the guys he had picked out so far were going to meet back at his house sometime next week after school. Did I want to be in the group? I was thrilled at the invitation. Driving home that night I laughed and sang "doo wop" all the way home.

The following week I drove up to Jan's after school. I pulled up in front of the house and noticed that Jan's car wasn't there. So I went up to the front door and knocked. This very pretty blonde lady answered the door. She introduced herself as Mrs. Berry, Jan's mom. She invites me in and offers me some cookies and milk. We sit in the kitchen. Within ten minutes she is asking for my advice on how to handle Jan. Shit, how am I supposed to know? I'm a teenager myself! Hmmm. Well, hadn't she ever heard the standard threat that had always worked at my house? It always worked on all my neighborhood pals, too. Why hadn't she ever heard of it? She had five other kids, Jan being the oldest. How could she not know? Well, I guess I'm going to have to be the one to provide her with this profound bit of reverse psychology.

"Well Mrs. Berry, just tell him if he doesn't abide by your rules, that this is your home and he is no longer welcome here, so please pack up your things and hit the road!" I was so proud to have shared this time-tested method to save their family unit!

"Oh, I can't do that," she exclaimed. I was shocked!

"Why not?" I asked.

"Because he would," she stated. "As a matter of fact, a year ago he left, went to San Francisco, dyed his hair black, lived in Golden Gate Park in a sleeping bag, and got a part-time job at a print shop." Well, scratch that idea!

About that time Jan showed up with some of the other guys and we retreated to the music room. Jan had picked out the song we were going to learn first. He put "Get a Job" on the turntable. That was one of my favorites, I knew it backwards and forwards. We all picked out a part. The moment of truth had arrived. We were going to sing this song without the record into the microphone and on to the tape. No shower room echo.

"Ah, but hold on," Jan announces. "I have found a way to create an echo effect by using both tape recorders at the same time. The vocals will go into one tape machine and then will be patched and transferred to the other machine and this will cause a slight delay, which has a quality that sounds very much like an echo. Let's do it and I'll show you."

We tried it and it worked. We sounded okay. Not great, but okay, for our first attempt. We experimented with placement around the microphone. Jan wasn't happy with the vocal quality. He blamed the cheap microphone. We needed an Electro-Voice microphone. Let's call it a day. Hey, let's take all the turkey 45s down the street to a hill overlooking the main road into Bel Air. The name of this game was Platter Golf. Jan would divide up all of the expendable 45s amongst us. We would launch our 45s towards the golf course, hoping to get our 45 on one of the greens below. The person to get the closest to the flag was the winner.

To this day I wonder if somewhere there is a groundskeeper who has quite a valuable old record collection! Or maybe someday someone might happen to excavate a bunch of old Five Satins or Mello-Kings' records from the gully just short of the golf course.

The next day Jan tells us to meet him at the lunchtime movie at our high school auditorium. We meet him there just a little after noon. We are all sitting in the front row when the lights go down and the movie starts. The movie is still running the titles when Jan gets up, walks to the stairs leading up to the stage, and disappears behind the screen. We can hear him bumping and clanking around in the dark behind the screen. We are all trying to control our laughter. The bumping and clanking stop. Minutes later Jan walks back into the auditorium from an outside door. He sits down for a few minutes, then stands up and says, "Let's go." Once outside he opens up his jacket. Stuck in his waistband is an Electro-Voice microphone. "Meet you all at my house after school," he says, and off he goes.

That afternoon, by the time we arrive at his house, he has the Electro-Voice microphone all hooked up and ready to go. After a few hours of recording, we all agree that we do sound better. Then we think, boy we would really sound better if we had a better set of speakers. A few days later I am in my homeroom class, and the teacher reads an announcement. It seems that over the weekend someone had stolen a pair of large green speakers. The speakers had been loaned to the school by our favorite science teacher, Mr. Farnum. That afternoon at our usual after-school practice, Jan can't wait for us to hear his new speakers. They sounded great and were an unusual color—green.

Our rehearsal did sound better, especially coming through our new green speakers. But Jan was still not completely happy. Our background vocals were pretty damn good, but the lead vocal didn't sound like the record. Well the record we were trying to copy was sung by a black group and the lead vocal was spot-on, and our lead vocalist just wasn't in the same league.

We were all sitting around in The Barons' usual spot in the quad during lunch the following day. Jan was still perplexed about how to overcome our lead singer problem. Then he spots the new kid. He is the only black student at our school, and he is sitting all by himself eating his lunch. Jan says he has found our new lead singer. When we ask how he could know without hearing him sing, Jan says all black guys can sing.

With that he got up and headed over to the kid. The kid, seeing Jan walking straight towards him wearing his Barons Club jacket, stares down at his lunch. This was starting to look like a scene out of *Westside Story* or *Rebel Without a Cause*. Jan is now standing right in front of him. Jan says, "Hey, what's your name?"

The kid slowly looks up and says, "I'm Chuck."

Jan says, "Hey Chuck, I'm Jan. Would you like to be in our group?" True story, I swear. And Jan was right, Chuck could sing. So he became our lead singer.

Now that we had all of the vocals down as good as we were ever going to get them, we started thinking about our stage presentation. We were used to Jan playing piano, but we really wanted him to be standing with the rest of us. Jan suggested that he could call his neighbor, Bruce Johnston, who was a good piano player. Maybe he would like to play with us. Bruce jumped at the chance to join us on stage.

And then the most important part—we need a name. Well, we were all Barons (except for Chuck and Bruce) so let's call ourselves The Barons. Now we were ready! Bring on the talent show.

The show went by so fast I barely remember it. We did three songs, each a little over two minutes long, so in eight minutes or so it was all over. Jan suggested that we meet at his house after school to plan the next phase of our alleged musical careers. "What musical careers are you talking about?" most of us wanted to know. The talent show was over, and there wouldn't be another one until next semester, and by that time we'd have graduated.

When I got to Jan's that afternoon, I was the only one to show up. "Where is everybody?" I asked. Jan said that Wally really wanted to be a pharmacist, John had met a special girl and wanted to spend more time with her after school, and Chuck was replacing the lead singer in The Del-Vikings. Wow! A group that already had hit records. I was flabbergasted!

"Chuck plays that one talent show with us and parlays that into becoming the new lead singer of The Del-Vikings, a group that's already hit it big," I said. "See Jan, that's what happens when you have a great lead singer, they get better offers and they bolt. That's fuckin' unreal." Jan gave me the same look that I got when I thought he owned a radio station. It seems in reality Chuck's mom had taken away the car keys until his grades improved.

"The story on Arnie is that he has gotten a part-time job after school, but he can come to practice a couple of days a week."

"Cool, but what are we practicing for?" I still wasn't exactly clear on that.

"We are going to make a record," Jan proclaimed. "We need to write some songs. I'll get some paper." I had never thought about writing a song. It just had never occurred to me. Of course, without a song you don't have anything.

We wrote down some subject matter ideas and some interesting tune titles. Jan had started writing a song called "Sally"—she lived up on the hill or something like that. So, for lack of anything better to work on, we tinkered around with that song.

After a couple of weeks we still had nothing better than the "Sally" song. Arnie and a few other guys dropped by one night and we all agreed that we needed some songwriting inspiration. Someone said, "Let's go to a topless bar!" They were called burlesque clubs in those days. Some of us had never been to a topless bar before, so we thought the inspiration would just come oozing out of us.

We drove to a very seedy part of downtown LA, looking for 548 South Main Street, where we found The New Follies Burlesk. And yes, someone spelled the word "Burlesk" in the advertising and even in the signage.

It was smoky, smelly, and filthy, but I loved it! I was going to see some tits. The lights went down. Out comes a pudgy girl in an ugly dress. She strips. She was even uglier with her clothes off. Not much inspiration so far. Now the headliner comes out, Jenny Lee "The Bazoom Girl," and she was something special. The old guys with the trench coats in their laps sitting in front of the stage start chanting, "Jenny Lee! Jenny Lee! Jenny Lee!" She was the star, and she was the one everyone was waiting for. We clapped and stamped on the floor.

The lights go down and the music starts. She slithers through the curtains. She's huge and the place goes nuts. She prances, dances, and teases. She finally flops those big ol' hooters out there for everyone to see. There's a near riot. She has tassels over her nipples, thank God, and she twirls them around and around. What an ugly sight, I thought.

"Pretty fuckin' great," says one of the guys to me.

"Oh, God, yes, an absolute dream girl," I reply, hiding my nausea. The old men in front are punctuating each bounce of her gazebos by shouting out "Bomp! Bomp! Bomp!" I was about to puke.

Jenny gives the audience one last glimpse of her butt before exiting the stage. I could count the pimples.

After the show we pile back into the car and drive back toward Jan's. Driving west on Sunset we pass through Hollywood, we go past Schwab's Drug Store and then the streets Crescent Heights and Doheny. Arnie has been duly inspired—he has already taken the "bomp, bomp, bomp" of the old men and is starting to build a song around it.

By the time we reach Dead Man's Curve, just above the UCLA practice field, the song "Jenny Lee" has some structure to it. I'm thinking I was more inspired by the drive back from downtown. Maybe we should do a song about driving on Sunset, or driving past the world famous Schwab's Drug Store, or driving through Dead Man's Curve. Nah, that's probably a stupid idea. The guys would laugh me out of the car. Back at Jan's Arnie and Jan go straight into the studio to work on the song while the rest of us went home—we had homework to do.

Over the next couple of weeks we would all at one time or another work on "Jenny Lee." Arnie sang lead, Jan sang the bass, and the rest of us sang some background harmony parts. Many times we were in Jan's studio at different times. Jan was a master at splicing tape. He would record a complete song maybe ten or fifteen times, sometimes days apart, even using different singers. He had a metronome to keep the tempo consistent. Then he would painstakingly cut a piece from take three, let's say, another piece from take six, two different pieces from take eleven, two notes from take five, and so on. When did this guy ever study? I know that's what you're thinking. We were all wondering the same thing.

Meanwhile I was getting ready to graduate from high school. I was a midterm student, a half a semester ahead of Jan and the other guys in the group. One day an Army recruiter came to our school to talk to the senior boys about joining the Army Reserve program. He told us that the Reserve program was being phased out soon, and we had better take advantage of it while we could—or face the possibility of being drafted sometime in the future. In the Army Reserve program, if we signed up while still in high school, we would only have to be in active duty for six months, but we would have to go to night meetings every other week for three years.

The world was relatively peaceful in 1958, so I thought it might be a smart idea to do it now and get it over with. Some of my non-singing buddies agreed, and a bunch of us signed up. I figured since I would graduate at the end of January, I'd have a month to play around, go to basic training in March when I turned eighteen, and be out in September, just in time to start college for the fall semester. When I told Jan what I was going to do, I got that "what a moron" look once again.

"We're working on a record! Why did you decide to do this now? Why now? We're almost finished," he said. I had been calculating the time that it would take to write and record the flip side to "Jenny Lee," then the time it would take to peddle the song. I just didn't think much would happen in the next six months. I mean, come on, a finished record, both sides with instruments, a recording contract, a management team. Nah, no way. "Don't worry about it," I told him. "I'll be back in time."

I was to leave for Fort Ord in Northern California on a Sunday morning, so Saturday was my last day in town. I wanted to spend it with my fairly new girlfriend, Cindy. Jan had invited me to go to a recording studio in Hollywood to make a demo record off of our garage tape, but I told him I had made other plans and I wouldn't have time to go to Hollywood with him. I ended up spending most of the day in the local mountains playing in the snow with my new girlfriend and some of my high school buddies that were also going to Fort Ord the next day.

That evening I returned home early to finish packing. The phone rings. It's Jan and he is very excited. He tells me he took the tape that we had made of the Jenny Lee song to a recording studio, and as he and an engineer were transferring the song from the tape to a lacquered disc in a small editing studio, a guy had appeared from out of nowhere. Said he heard the song through the door, and recognizing the unprofessional quality of the recording, surmised it was a novice attempt for audition purposes. I guess he was right. He introduced himself as Joe Lubin, president of Arwin Records, a company owned by Doris Day and her husband Marty Melcher. Mr. Lubin goes on to tell Jan that if Jan allows him to finish the record and put it out, that Jan and his partners will be bigger than the Everly Brothers! I almost dropped the phone. Nobody could be bigger than the Everly Brothers, I thought. This guy is a lunatic!

Jan then asks me if I'm still planning to go to Fort Ord. Hell, yes, I'm going to Fort Ord! Do I have a choice? Hey, just call them and tell them that you have changed your mind, or something like that, he tells me. Be sure to mention the Everly Brothers thing! Well, I still thought nothing much would happen in six months, so I told Jan I would be back in LA after basic training, in just two months, and we could reevaluate everything then. He hangs up, ticked off, and I go back to packing.

The next day, six of us high school buddies fly up to the Monterey Airport in Northern California where we are picked up by a military bus and driven to the military base at Fort Ord. We are welcomed, and then marched off to the barbershop. I didn't want to give the Army barber any satisfaction in cutting off my long—by fifties standards, of course—hair, so I had gotten a haircut a few days before from my regular barber. The Army barber was not to be denied. He still wanted his shot, so I got a second haircut.

That night all six of us got together, had a few beers, and tried to figure out how we had gotten into this mess. For a bunch of upper middle class eighteen-year-olds from West Los Angeles, this Fort Ord place was truly bizarre. Over the next few days, it just got weirder and weirder. Nothing made much sense. The people in charge hadn't a clue, and on top of that the guys most directly involved with us could barely speak English. They were Asian, but what kind of Asian was a mystery to us.

We started to realize that we were a lot smarter than most of the guys in charge—a scary thought since up until that time we had thought that anybody older than us was automatically smarter than us. Only a few days in the Army dispelled that notion. We decided to make up our own rules and try to get away with anything we could. Within a month we had forged Class A passes getting us on and off the base any time we wanted. We also had hidden civilian clothes and other contraband on the base.

Then one morning, one of my high school buddies, Bill Young, was listening to his portable radio when he picks up one of the local rock 'n' roll stations. All of a sudden he runs up to me with his radio and says excitedly, "Listen to this!" Oh, shit. I can't believe it! I'm hearing "Jenny Lee" on the radio! It sounds great. There are now instruments added on to the record, but everything else seems to be the same.

I am holding my breath at the end of the record in anticipation of hearing our group name, The Barons, over the radio. The last "Jenny Lee" sound is over, and the disc jockey says, "That's a new big hit, 'Jenny Lee,' by Jan & Arnie."

I just about died. Here I am in this hellhole, and worse yet, by my choice, and my musical buddies back home have a real hit record. I really did fuck up. It was right there and I blew it. This has to be a nightmare. I'm going to wake up to the sound of a loud obnoxious platoon sergeant telling us to get up and fall into formation for an inspection. Oh, God. It's not a dream. I am awake and I just heard our song on the radio, and it was pretty obvious I was no longer involved.

After breakfast we were to do about an hour and a half march to the firing range. My mind was racing. Well, maybe they are saving my place in the group, and when I get out we will change the name back to The Barons. Wait, why would they make such a radical change in the name when the name Jan & Arnie was already established? Sure, that makes sense. Well, maybe we will just add my first name to theirs—Jan, Arnie & Dean. Yeah, that would be the best solution. Who the hell am I kidding? Why would they cut the pie three ways? It's obvious they don't need me, they don't need anybody else! They have a hit record with just the two of them. Holy shit, I really did blow it!

I'm marching in the fog and in the rain to the firing range with a bunch of idiots, including me, that actually signed up for this, and Jan and Arnie are probably flying off, first class of course, to Philadelphia to be on *American Bandstand*. I guess I now know how Pete Best, the original drummer for the Beatles, felt—or should I say, was going to feel.

Okay. I've got to come up with a plan. Yeah, I got it, a phone call. That's what I'll do. I'll call Jan tonight after dinner. Damn. Hope he is home and not out hobnobbing with Elvis, or the Everly Brothers, or Frankie Avalon, or on a date with Ann Margaret or Annette Funicello, or somebody like that. By the way, even though I was somewhat distracted at the firing range, I still fired expertly with both the M1 and the Carbine. Hey, maybe there was something new in my future! Maybe I could be a hit man, or mercenary, or double agent, or Phil Spector's bodyguard. Hmmm.

That evening I called Jan from a base pay phone, and low and behold he was home.

"Hey, Jan, how's it going?"

"Fine."

"How's school?"

"Fine."

"Playing any volleyball?"

"Oh, a little."

"Jan, I heard 'Jenny Lee' on the radio!"

"Oh, yeah, the record came out. It's doing very well."

"Yes, it sounded great, but you know at the end of the record they said it was by Jan & Arnie, not The Barons."

"Well, that's because it is by Jan & Arnie, not The Barons. We had to re-sing the recording and you weren't around. I called your mom, and she said she would have to write to you to call me since you didn't have a phone. So we just did it ourselves. Sorry. I told you not to go."

"Yeah, you did. But are you sure that's not one of the vocals that I sang on?" I asked, hoping that maybe it was and that in a moment of weakness Jan would fess up and say yes it was me in the background, because I was damn sure I heard myself.

"No, Dean. We re-sang it after you left. I'm sorry you weren't here, but that's the way it goes. Give me a call when you come home on leave. I've got to go now. See ya."

It was now official. Jesus, I really did blow it. Tomorrow I'd better really concentrate on that grenade launcher.

Another month goes by. "Jenny Lee" is all over the radio and the six of us from University High are quasi celebrities just because we went to the same school as Jan and Arnie. Also, by this time we have snuck a car onto base and have forged officers' identification cards allowing us to eat and drink any time day or night in the exclusive officers' club. We also have special passes allowing us to leave the base on Tuesday and Thursday night in civilian clothes to attend Masonic functions in Carmel and Monterey. We never made it to any of the Masonic functions, but we did play volleyball in Carmel, hung in some fun bars in Salinas, and had some great seafood dinners in Monterey. We now had four months done— only two months to go when we would finally get a three-day pass, enough time to go home to LA.

My first full day at home, I called Jan and told him I had a date that night, but I would like to drop by and say hi if he had the time.

He said he was working on the follow-up to "Jenny Lee" and I was welcome to drop by. The drive up to his house was strange. So much had happened in the last four months. Those carefree high school days were indeed over. The age of innocence was slowly fading away.

When I walked into the old studio you could cut the tension with a knife. Jan and Arnie were sitting on the piano bench facing the piano and an older guy was pacing directly behind them. They all glanced at me when I walked in, but then went back to their work. There appeared to be some problem. All three seemed to be stressed. I was very uncomfortable. I hoped that someone would break the ice by saying something to me.

After what seemed to be a very long time, the older guy looked at me and said they were right in the middle of trying to finish a song and that having a visitor was distracting. So I got up and left. As I drove back up that long driveway, the same one that had so many glorious memories, I was overwhelmed with the now very obvious fact that it would never be the same. The music room used to be the club house, the place that was always fun. Everybody had been welcome.

Sunday night the young warriors all piled into our car and drove the five hours back to Fort Ord. Over the next couple of months we heard the new Jan & Arnie record, though not as often as we had heard "Jenny Lee." Some of the biggest hits on the radio at the time were "My True Love" by Jack Scott and "When Will You Be Mine?" by the Kalen Twins. I had hoped to run into some guys in the Army who had an interest in singing, but I never did. So we spent most of our time and energy trying to beat the military system.

By this time we had completed basic training and had also completed our schooling. Some of my friends went to truck driving school, or clerk typing school, radio operating school, weapons maintenance school, and three of us had gone to cooking school. It turned out to be a great gig. We were never hungry, cold, or dirty.

Upon graduation from cooking school we were assigned to different places. The lucky guys stayed at Fort Ord. The unlucky guys ended up in the Deep South, where it was hot and humid.

I was assigned to an advanced infantry special unit right there at Fort Ord. Upon arrival, my sergeant asked me if I was permanent party. "Of course," I replied, although I hadn't a clue what that meant. But hey, it couldn't hurt? He gave me a room number and told me to put my stuff in that room and then report to him in the mess hall. "Yes, sir!" I replied and off I went.

When I find the room I am surprised to see that it is a small room with two beds. There doesn't seem to be anyone else staying in the room. Damn. I have my own room. How cool is that? I go to the mess hall to find Sergeant Miller. He is a big black guy, an Army career cook. He seems okay. He tells me we are preparing to go out on bivouac for a couple of weeks and that he has no time to train me right now, so he wants me to be the head of the kitchen police, aka KP. He says that since I am permanent party—there are those words again—he is in no big hurry to train me. He says that we will have plenty of time for that after we get back from bivouac. All right, that sounds okay to me. Take your time, sergeant.

So for a couple of weeks I would show up after breakfast, show the guys on kitchen police duty what to do—washing dishes, peeling potatoes, or cleaning out those disgusting grease traps. Then I would make my own breakfast, usually steak and eggs, while I kept an eye on the KPs.

Lunch was basically the same routine. Some of my old school buddies were driving the trucks that would bring a lot of our supplies and I would invite them to stay for lunch. I would cook them a custom lunch from my personal food stash. Then to top off our lunch I'd make them all hot fudge sundaes for dessert. And of course I'd ask the KPs to remove our plates for us.

We finally went on bivouac into the field for two weeks. This was under combat conditions for the troops, but not for us, the cooks. At one point it crossed my mind that if this were a real war it would be a hellish nightmare because the people making the life-and-death decisions were incompetent buffoons. God, we were lucky that this was just pretend.

By the time we got back from bivouac I would only have about a week left of active duty. My girlfriend, my truck, my first day in college, and the thought that maybe Jan & Arnie might need me—these were the first things on my mind.

A few weeks later, we were back at the barracks when Sergeant Miller called me into his office. He was pissed.

"Torrence, I just got your discharge orders! I thought you said you was permanent party?"

"Well, I thought I was permanent party at least for a while. How permanent did you think I meant?"

"Regular Army permanent is what I thought."

"Aw, Sarge, we had a semantics problem. Sorry about that."

"Fuck yo semantics! Go get your discharge physical and while you are at it, Mr. Permanent Party, get a goddamn haircut. You look like a pussy rock 'n' roll faggot. When you're done, you get your skinny ass back here on the double and I will work you till the minute you leave here, you hear me soldier?"

"Yes, sir!"

As I placed my order for a banana split at the base Dairy Queen, I was trying to figure out how to stretch the discharge physical out to take up most of the day. By the time I got to the hospital for my physical I had a plan.

"Sir," I said to one of the paper pushers, "someone typed up my serial number wrong, it should be FR19599207 but on this form it says FR19599206. What should I do?"

"Well, Private, you'll have to take this form back to the Administration Office, a short bus ride to the other side of the base, and have them retype your serial number on the DFE-1B form."

"Damn inconvenient, sir!"

"Sorry about that soldier."

So it was back to the Dairy Queen for a butterscotch sundae and to read the newspaper and catch up on the sports news. After a couple of hours, I returned to the hospital with the original DFE-1B form.

"Boy, what a hassle that was, sir!" I told the paper pusher. The physical went smoothly, so now it was time to head back to the barracks, and I was hoping that Sergeant Miller had gone home for the day. He had! Actually I felt bad that I didn't get a chance to say good-bye to Sergeant Miller. He was a really nice guy. He was going to retire soon and was looking forward to that day. I hope it all worked out for him.

On September 7, 1958, at 7 a.m., the bus picked up all of the Los Angeles guys and took us to the Monterey airport. We were free at last. Free at last, hallelujah!

God it was great to be home. It was early September. I had about two weeks before I started my first semester at Santa Monica City College. The school was seven minutes from the beach! Man, we were going to have a great time. Football season was also starting and I was looking forward to finding some weekend sandlot games to play in. I called some of my old high school buddies to find out if there were any games being played. I was thrilled to find out they had just started playing every Sunday morning at Palisades High School football field, and most of the same old guys were all showing up. It was going to be great to see all the old gang again.

Sunday finally arrived and I was pumped. I jumped in the truck, headed up Beverly Glen, and turned left on Sunset. What a gorgeous California day! It was sunny, the sky was blue, and "Teenager in Love" was playing on the radio. My truck had a new coat of wax and I had fixed up my old Adidas football shoes with some tape. This is going to be one hell of a day.

Arriving at the field, I was very surprised to see the turnout. It was like a homecoming. Holy shit, even Jan was here! Why wasn't he on tour with the Dick Clark Caravan of Stars? Or rehearsing for *The Ed Sullivan Show*? Or sailing with Ann Margaret? Shit, I don't believe it. He still plays ball. What a stud. "Hey, Jan, good to see ya!"

"Hey, Dean, did you go AWOL?"

"Oh, no. I'm finished with active duty. I start school next week."

He said his first day of classes at UCLA were also next week. Why was he going to school? I thought he was a rock-and-roll star with lots of exciting things to do. Plus, with all that money he was making, why would he need to go to school at all? He should be able to retire. Somebody yelled "Let's play!" So we did.

After the game we all went to the beach and did some body surfing. As we sat together against a warm cement wall separating the beach from the parking lot and soaked up the last rays of the sun, we talked about all the different things we were going to do. Some of the guys already had jobs, some were in the process of getting ready to look for a job, and the rest of us were going on to college. A couple of guys were going to UCLA and a couple were going to USC and a few more were going to be joining me at Santa Monica City College.

When the sun started to set we decided to call it a day. Jan asked me where I was going and I said, "Home, I guess." I really didn't have anything planned. So he said, "Wanna come up to my house and work on some songs?" I was stunned.

"What about Arnie?"

"He no longer seems to be interested in making music."

Damn, I knew this was going to be a bitchin' day. "Let's go," I said. I didn't want him to change his mind.

2

"BABY TALK"

{1959}

followed Jan's turquoise and white fuel-injected '57 Chevy up Chautauqua, right onto Sunset, and past Palisades High School towards Bel Air. My mind was racing. Reality-check time. Why would Arnie not be interested in making records, performing on stage, being on TV, meeting all those chicks, and making all that money? I don't get it! Something's not right, and there is no way in hell he is just going to hand me the baton, pat me on the back, give me a big smile, and say, "It's now your turn, buddy. Have lots of fun!" What is going on here? Now I'm starting to worry.

As I drive I'm thinking, Arnie will probably already be up at Jan's with their record producer or the record company president. They will tell Jan they have a binding contract and that he has to record with Arnie for the next two years, like it or not. "Dean, you may be excused," they'll say. Or, maybe Jan had bludgeoned Arnie to death right there in the music room, next to the piano. The cops have just found his body in a pool of blood, and they will arrest Jan as soon as he pulls into the driveway. No, wait a minute, Jan is way too smart to show up and get arrested. Oh shit, now I get it. He is setting me up—he's going to frame me. It was obvious that I had the perfect motive to whack Arnie.

Something is going to fuck this up, I just know it.

We pull into the driveway. Just the usual cars. So far so good. We walk into the music room. Nobody is on the floor. I look around. Jan's record collection has doubled in size. There are framed Jan & Arnie gold records on the wall and a brand-new Telefunken microphone hanging over the piano. Other than that, it hadn't changed that much.

Jan played some songs that he was working on and that he had put on tape. Then we listened to some 45s he had just gotten in the mail, hoping for some inspiration. Then it was time to sit down at the piano bench together to see what we had. We sang some standards, then dabbled with some original tunes he was working on, none of which were memorable. But we seemed to have fun.

Oh, shit! I remembered that I was supposed to call my girlfriend Cindy a couple of hours ago and that we were maybe going to get together that night. But I didn't want to jeopardize my maybe onetime only shot at getting the chance to be Jan's new partner. Maybe he was auditioning me and had others in mind as well. So I'd better seize this moment for all it was worth. I called Cindy and told her I wouldn't be able to see her that night but that I would call her the next day. She was disappointed that we wouldn't be getting together, but happy to hear that I was getting involved in making music with Jan again. I have always wondered if she sensed that this was the beginning of the end of our relationship. Jan was a very controlling type of guy and would not like to have a partner that was influenced by anyone but him. And I am sure she knew that. A career in music was going to take full concentration. There would be no time for petty outside interests. Sweet dreams, Cindy. I'll call you tomorrow.

Jan and I sang and talked for a couple more hours. Arnie's name never came up. Jan said the record company had some demonstration tapes of song possibilities and record ideas, and that he would pick them up and we could listen to them tomorrow night. He thought maybe we could find a hit song amongst them.

The next night we went through the tapes. Most of the songs were pathetically lame. We picked one and worked on it for a couple of hours, then finally gave up. It was never going to be any better than an average song. Jan said he knew a black guy that swept the floor at his barbershop who had formed a group and that they had some original songs. He said he would ask him about bringing his group up to the house, offer to record them, and see if they had any songs we could steal—uh, use. Jan knew I had a part-time job at Robert's Liquor Store. He told me to get some liquor for the guys in the group. Jan thought they would probably work for booze.

The next day I was to work a couple of hours restocking the shelves at the liquor store. I was figuring out how to come up with six bottles of booze. Jan assumed I either had enough money to buy it or I would steal it. Well, I didn't have the money, and besides I was still underage, so there was no way my boss would sell it to me anyway. But I couldn't let Jan down—so I stole the booze. Sorry, Jack, but as you can now see, it went to a great cause.

The guys from Jan's barbershop finally did show up. We grouped them around our only microphone, turned on the tape recorder, and they indeed sang their butts off. But it was the same old problem as it usually is—the songs. The songs were average at best. Ah, but they did sing the shit out of them.

We gave them their booze and off they went. Then we tinkered with a couple of their songs but nothing materialized, so we called it a night. The record company was now calling Jan, asking for the next single. Jan told them he was working on it, he just needed a little more time. They knew nothing about Jan's plan to replace Arnie with me. We decided to pick the best songs we had so we would have something to work on to keep the record company quiet. Meanwhile, we would continue to search for better quality recording material. We worked for a couple of nights on one song. It was one we had gotten from Arwin Records, a song that they thought had potential. It sucked big time. We finally gave up on it.

Then we went back to work on a song that Jan had started. I added some parts, came up with an interesting falsetto line, noting at the same time that none of the Jan & Arnie records had falsetto parts. Gee, our own signature!

We took the song as far as we could. It would at least show the record company that we were capable of executing a song from beginning to end. Jan called Arwin Records the next day and made an appointment with them to bring in a possible follow-up to the single. It would also be the first time they would hear about the personnel change. Would they be receptive to this surprising bit of news? It was kind of like Stan Laurel going into Roach Studios one day and announcing, "Oh, by the way, Hardy is out, and meet my new partner, Chad Ochocinco!" Laurel & Ochocinco—it kinda has a ring to it, don't you think? Well, why wouldn't they be interested in this new configuration? Our singing was about the same. Arnie had a very unique sounding voice, while my voice, in comparison, sounded fairly average. On the other hand, I had a lot more vocal range, including falsetto, which he didn't have. Visually, Jan and Arnie were also a study in contrasts. One a tall, waspy, blonde kid— the other a short, dark-complexioned Jewish kid. Jan and Dean had what I called visual continuity.

Jan & Dean were almost like two bookends: two tall, waspy blondes with the same body type. The guys that we were going to ultimately be compared to were the Everly Brothers, who could have passed for twins. They obviously had visual continuity. A lot of people have a hard time getting beyond the fact that something just doesn't look right. With that said, I was sure Arwin Records would find the new partnership intriguing.

We went to the meeting in Beverly Hills dressed in our newest jeans and most colorful short-sleeved shirts. Jan introduced me to Joe Lubin, the record producer, and Marty Melcher, the record company president. "Dean is Arnie's replacement," he announced.

They looked shocked. After a few uncomfortable moments, Jan matter-of-factly tells them this is the way it was supposed to be in the first place, and that our partnership just got sidetracked, so here is our tape. Check it out.

They quietly listened to the tape. After some small talk they said they had another meeting to go to and they would call later. Holy shit, I don't believe it. There was no positive reaction to us at all! Jan said he would call them later and straighten everything out. I was sure they were going to tell Jan it's you and Arnie or adios. How would Jan react to that? There was still the real possibility that I could be shown the door once again. I didn't hear from Jan that day and I was really worried. I couldn't even eat.

The next afternoon Jan called and said we needed to get together. I was so scared driving up to his house, I was sure this was it. He was waiting for me in the music room. He said he had talked to the record company, and they wanted him to stay with Arnie or they were no longer interested. So he said he told them to fuck off. Jesus Christ, it's official, Arnie is out and I am in. But then again, big fuckin' deal. Without a record company we had nothing.

I couldn't believe it. Jan had had three records with them—one went gold, one charted, and one failed. Not a bad track record for an eighteen-year-old. It wasn't like he was a burned-out, old has-been. Jan said not to worry. We were better off being released from that shitty record company. How could we be better off being dumped? God damn it. It was so close! Now it looked like I would never get the chance to see my name on a record.

"I've got an idea," Jan said. "We need a manager." I hadn't a clue why we would need a manager, especially when there wasn't much to manage.

Jan recalled meeting these two guys at a concert he did with Arnie last summer. Sam Cook was the headliner on that show and these two young guys were on his management team. And guess what, they were songwriters, too. Jan had kept their business card.

Jan finds the card. "Yeah, that's the one guy's name, Lou Adler. Let's give him a call," he says. Jan gets Lou on the phone and explains our situation and asks him if he has any interest in meeting with us. He said he's very interested and would like to get together that night, if possible. Jan was very excited about getting together with Lou and his partner. He said that they were really groovy guys—smart and talented.

Lou and his partner arrived at Jan's right on time. They walked into the music room and seemed very happy to see Jan again. Then they introduced themselves to me.

"Hi! I'm Lou Adler."

"And I'm Herb Alpert." Man, they were well-dressed.

We talked about Sam Cook and the song, "Wonderful World" that both Lou and Herbie had written. Then we played them our song, admitting that the material was weak, but that we thought our execution was pretty good and they agreed. It was then decided that we should give it a go together. We all knew what we needed was "that song," so we decided to start the search and go from there. Lou said that he had a bunch of demo records at his office and he would start plowing through them the next day.

We all shook hands and off they went. Jan explained that Lou was more of the businessman and that Herbie was the musician, but that both guys were very creative and had lots of vision. We were lucky to have them on our team. A couple of days later Lou called Jan and wanted to get together to play some songs for us, so we decided to meet that night up at Jan's.

Man, do they dress well! I thought. Lou and Herbie were wearing Continental suits, thin ties, cool tie tacks, gold rings, and European shoes. They brought along a few songs on tape and a couple of 45s. The songs on the tape had been submitted to Sam Cook, so they were mostly ballads. Really nice songs, but not our style. The 45s were small independent record companies' newest releases that would probably never see the light of day no matter how good they were. Most of them were performed by black artists, so even if they became hits, they would most likely only be played on the rhythm and blues stations.

The average white teenagers were not listening to those radio stations. In some cases, white teenage kids were not even permitted to listen to those kinds of stations at home. I remember having to sneak out of the house if my mom was home to go to my neighborhood buddy, Frank McCoy's house, to listen to Hunter Hancock's radio show. Frank was the only kid in the neighborhood being raised by a single mom. She had a full-time job so he was often home alone. So if we wanted to listen to black musicians, we had to go to Frank's house.

One of the 45s that Lou had brought up to Jan's caught our attention. It had doo-wops. It was cute. It was simple. It had a catchy melody.

"Hey, Lou. What's the name of that record?" I asked.

"It's called 'Baby Talk' by an unknown group called the Laurels, and it's on a very small independent record company."

"Let's work on this song," I said to Jan. Jan wanted to do the cool low bomps and "dip di did i dip" parts and I was to sing the lead. We would sing the chorus together in harmony, and I was to come up with a falsetto on the end. Yeah, that seemed like it would work. We have a song! Praise the Lord, we have a song!

For the next two or three weeks we recorded twenty similar versions of "Baby Talk." Jan would spend hours upon hours cutting verse one from take four, verse two from take eight, the first chorus from take three, the third verse from take twelve, and so on. The opening bomps were edited in and edited out numerous times until just the right combination was found. The end bomps and falsetto came from yet another take. Our final master tape done in the garage studio had to stay in tempo even with all those edits. This was not easy to accomplish. This garage studio tape would have only two voices and a piano on it when we were all done. Herb Alpert had written the arrangements for the rest of the instruments. Herb and Lou then contacted the musicians and booked a recording studio. Meanwhile, Jan and I threw together the flip side, "Jeanette Get Your Hair Done." It was a novelty song, and clearly not an A-side.

We showed up at the recording session one cool LA night in April 1959. Herbie had already laid out the sheet music for the musicians. The leader was a guy named Ernie Freeman, and they were all members of a successful studio band. These guys were the cream of the crop. Ernie was the keyboard player, Renee Hall was the guitarist, Earl Palmer played drums, Plaz Johnson played sax, and Bill Pitman played the standup bass. They all wore earphones so they could listen to our vocal tape—then they were going to attempt to play along with it. This was absolutely ass-backwards to what they were used to doing. Standard recording procedure was, and for the most part still is, to record the instruments first, then the singers will sing along to the instrumental track until they get the take they like. These guys were thoroughly amused by our new technique, but they were professionals and their tempo was impeccable and precise. Our tape, which sounded reasonably in tempo to us, sounded like a train wreck to them. But they laughed their way through it, and in the end it all worked out fine.

We loved it. The finished record sounded great. We all had high expectations. Herbie and Lou said they had already quit their jobs and were now prepared to work full-time on our project. I remember being both shocked and flattered that they believed in us enough to give up real paychecks. But how would they pay their bills without their day jobs? I was worried that they were being a little overly optimistic.

A week or so later Herbie and Lou announced that they had gotten us a record deal with Dore Records. This relatively new independent company was just coming off a giant hit, "To Know Him Is to Love Him" by the Teddy Bears. The record company had credibility, clout, and money—just what we needed. Herbie and Lou had now formed their own new management company, Herbie Lou Productions. Look out, world!

Then Lou announces that he is getting married. I didn't even know he had a girlfriend! Why would he get married now? We needed his full attention, plus he had just quit his day job. How in the world was he going to support this new wife? Just a couple of days after he gets married, Lou says we need to go shopping for outfits for the stage and for taking photos. You know, like the suits he and Herb wear. We also need sweaters, shirts, ties, socks, and shoes. Hey, Lou, I don't have that kind of money. Lou says not to worry, he would advance me the money. How's he going to do that? I thought.

We all met up at Lou's new Hollywood apartment. We met his beautiful new bride Deanna, and checked out all of his brand-new furniture. Then Lou said it was time to go shopping so we should hit the road. We walked down to his garage.

"Well, what do you think of our new company car?" Christ, he has a brand-new white Ford Thunderbird with a beautiful white top. We get in and he drives us downtown to the LA Garment District.

Lou has our whole wardrobe thought out. We buy more clothes that day than I had ever bought before, or come to think of it, since! On the way back to his apartment, Lou says we should have promotional copies of "Baby Talk" in a few days and once we have them we will get dressed up in our new suits and take the record to the number one rock station in LA, KFWB. Lou says he has a friend there, B. Mitchell Reed, one of the top disc jockeys in LA. Shit,

I couldn't wait to see a real 45 with a real record company label with my name on it.

The day finally arrived. I was very nervous about seeing a real record with my name on it. I didn't care what happened after that, I just wanted to have that record—a tangible thing that proved I had sung on a real record. I didn't care about anything more than that.

We drove to the record company to get our copies. I can vividly remember the overwhelming feeling I had when I actually held a record that was mine. It was beautiful. The label was blue, the vinyl was shiny black, and my name was spelled right. I couldn't wait to take it home to show it to my mom and dad. A few days later I started thinking about how cool it would be to hear "Baby Talk" on the radio. Just at least once. I wouldn't care if it ever got played again after that. Really, just one play would really mean it was taken seriously.

Lou called to tell me that we actually had an appointment to take the record to KFWB, the most important rock-and-roll station in Los Angeles. He told me exactly what to wear, and how to act. We met at Lou's the next day and from there drove to KFWB. We met with the program director who listened to our record. It was decided that "Baby Talk" would debut on the B. Mitchell Reed nighttime radio show. It would be part of a segment he called "Voice Your Choice." This was a part of his show where he played new records and the listeners were asked to call in and voice their choice of their favorite new record from the bunch. A winner would be crowned each night and would then go head-to-head with any new record the following night. I couldn't wait to hear our record on the radio. I hurried all the way home. I called all of my friends. My parents called all of their friends. We asked everybody to please call in. We needed their votes.

It seemed like forever until his show came on, and another forever until he played our record. Oh, shit, it sounded so good! I got chills, I broke out in a sweat, I almost threw up. I was a mess. Some of the other new records were also very good. I had no idea who would win. Mitch would wait until the end of his show to announce the winner and play it one more time.

All of a sudden we hear, "And the winner is . . . 'Baby Talk' by Jan & Dean." Holy shit! We won! I was bouncing off the walls.

The next day Jan came to my house to pick me up. He wanted to drive into Hollywood and check on any sales information he could analyze. The main stop would be at Wallichs Music City, the first mega record store of its day. This store was very important in terms of reporting record sales to the two most important record charts: Billboard and Cash Box. I followed Jan through the store straight to the 45 record single section. Jan knew exactly where the record would be. Well, actually, they were in alphabetical order. But still he knew almost without looking because his previous Jan & Arnie records were in the first place in the J section. Having the letter "A" after the "J" helped a lot to keep us there. And replacing "Arnie" with "Dean" obviously didn't affect our placement. Luckily, there were no "Jan & Arnie" records left to confuse the issue.

Jan pulled up the title index card with our name on it. It had a notation on it of the amount of records ordered and the date. Jan pointed out to me that they had ordered fifty records the day before. Then he proceeded to count the records in our section. Thirty-eight records were still there. "Hey, we sold twelve records in less than a day," he said. That was really good. Then he took about five records and spread them around into other people's sections, hoping that nobody would notice. We then left the store.

That night, "Baby Talk" was played as the Voice Your Choice champ from the night before. Then some other new releases were played. Damn, if we could only win just one more time that's all I would ever need. Really. That would prove it—that it was not just a fluke.

And the winner for the second night in a row was . . . "Baby Talk!" Okay, that really did it for me. If nothing else happens, I'll be content.

The next day Jan and I both had classes all day. But late that afternoon we went back to Music City. We were down to eleven records! So we spread another five or six around and left. That night the reigning champ, "Baby Talk" went head-to-head with the new competition. Wow! We won again!

The next afternoon we were back at Music City. It looked to me like they must have found the records we had stashed around the store, because there appeared to be more records in our section than there were yesterday. Jan looked at the title index card. "Fuckin' great!" he said. "They restocked a hundred records this morning, and that's a lot!" Now there are forty-one left. That's fifty-nine records in less than a day. We spread a few more around in other people's bins and left.

Then we dropped by the record company to report the sales. Everyone was pleased with the Los Angeles market, but nothing much was happening elsewhere. We decided to keep calling the B. Mitchell Reed Show because every time we won the Voice Your Choice contest, there were more sales at Music City. The more sales we could rack up gave us a better chance to make the KFWB Top 40, which would give us a lot more credibility nationwide. There was also the possibility that if we were on the KFWB Top 40 that we might get to play on *American Bandstand*, and that would mean that we were for real.

B. Mitchell Reed introduced "Baby Talk" that evening as once again the reigning champ for the fourth night in a row, and he added that if "Baby Talk" won that night, making it five in a row, then that would tie the record "Donna" by Richie Valens for the most consecutive wins. And the winner was ... "Baby Talk."

The following day we hit Music City again. Holy crap, look at all those records! They had restocked again. This time two hundred records. Jan counted again. After he finished counting he said, "Let's get out of here!" In the parking lot I asked Jan why he hadn't done our usual record spreading. He smiled and opened his jacket. He had a stack of at least forty records under his armpit. Gulp!

That night was the big night on KFWB. If we won Voice Your Choice again, we would have the record with six in a row. Man, now that would really mean something, I thought. If we could only win one more time, we could be in the history books. That's all I would ever need. I would really really be content. And the winner was ... "Baby Talk!" The new Voice Your Choice record holder. Yeah! Okay, now that really did it for me. Yes, I know I said that before but this really was all I needed.

Lou called the next day to tell us that we were cracking the KFWB sales chart next week at #36. This was going to help a lot. Music City also had a weekly chart and we were also debuting on that one as well. Jan said that he had a class that afternoon and early evening so we didn't do our usual Music City raid.

And oh, yeah, that night we won the Voice Your Choice KFWB award for the seventh night in a row. Later that evening, Jan called to say he couldn't help himself, and he had made a late-night raid with two high school buddies. Between them they had stolen more than seventy-five records. Then they raided another record store on the way home and took every "Baby Talk" record they had.

The following day I called Lou just to say hi. Somewhere in the conversation I commented on how unbelievable it was that we had won B. Mitchell Reed's Voice Your Choice a record seven times in a row, and that people were going to start thinking he was working for us or something.

"Well, he does," Lou said.

I said, "No, really, Lou."

He said, "Yes, really!" I was shocked. B. Mitchell Reed working for us? Jan stealing records. Friends and relatives calling in. Was anyone really interested in "Baby Talk" besides us? Lou explained that actually B. Mitchell Reed had signed a management agreement with Lou, so realistically Lou worked for B. Mitchell Reed and Jan & Dean as a manager. We were represented by the same person. Conflict of interest? Probably, but Lou made it clear that "Baby Talk" was winning each night without any help from B. Mitchell Reed. Yeah, but all of the calls were from us, or relatives, or friends. Lou pointed out that the record was getting many hundreds of legitimate calls and that it was a hit. I hoped he was right.

That night we won again for the eighth night in a row. It was starting to get embarrassing. Later Jan and I raided Music City again. The following day we got our first look at a printed KFWB Top 40 chart with "Baby Talk" listed at #36. Lou said that these charts would be sent to all the top rock stations in the United States. Also, Dick Clark had had Jan & Arnie on his *American Bandstand* show, and said that if "Baby Talk" showed some chart action he would be glad to play it on his daytime dance show. This would be a major breakthrough nationally for "Baby Talk." Man, if I could only hear "Baby Talk" on *American Bandstand,* just once. That would really be all I needed. That would verify that we were not just a funky garage band but a real rock music entity worthy of having a play on *American Bandstand.* If nothing else happened after that, so be it. I would be content with just that. Yeah, sure.

June 8, 1959, *Billboard Magazine,* one of the most important music industry publications, reviewed "Baby Talk." It was kind of negative, as I remember. A couple of days later we got confirmation that Dick Clark was going to debut "Baby Talk" on the rating part of his show. That was the part of the show where he would play the new records, and some selected kids would give the new record a rating score and a winner would be crowned. Uh-oh. We didn't have any relatives dancing on *American Bandstand*. Lou didn't manage Dick Clark. Nothing could be stolen or manipulated by us. We might be in trouble.

Meanwhile, we were finally dethroned on B. Mitchell Reed's show, thank God. But we did move up quite nicely on the next KFWB chart. The debut of "Baby Talk" on *American Bandstand* was a very exciting day. My parents, neighbors, and friends all gathered around our little black-and-white TV. Hearing Dick Clark introduce our record and say our names made me break out in a sweat. I got goose bumps and my hands went cold. The *Bandstand* kids danced, smiled, and seemed to like the record. Then came the moment of truth. Some Italian teenagers from Philly held our careers in the palms of their hands. I held my breath.

A couple of kids leaned towards Dick Clark's microphone and said, "We liked the beat. We gave it a 98." A cheer went up around the TV. "Baby Talk" ended up the winner. Would this mean he would play the record the next day? Would this mean that Dick Clark might let us perform the record on his television show? Stay tuned.

All the relatives called with congratulations. It was a great day. Then Lou called the following morning to report that just one play on *American Bandstand* had already caused some very significant national record orders, and that there was even more good news— Dick Clark was going to play the record again that day, and that there was some serious talk about us flying to Philadelphia to perform on *American Bandstand*! I about fainted!

I had a couple of classes that day so I would have to cut one to get home in time to see *Bandstand*. Man, it was weird. I couldn't tell any of my college friends I was cutting class to go home to watch *American Bandstand*. The Dick Clark show was thought of as a teenagers show, way beneath the dignity of a college student.

College students were way too sophisticated to be listening to rock 'n' roll. They were into jazz or folk music—you know, Kingston Trio, or Peter, Paul and Mary—music with profound messages. "Baby Talk" wasn't quite in that category.

We all gathered around the TV. "Baby Talk" was once again introduced and played. The kids danced. This was great! We were for real. About a week later Jan picked me up and we went to the beach together. As we drove, we were listening to KFWB. On came "Baby Talk." We turned it up. Was this totally bitchin' or what? Driving in Jan's turquoise, fuel-injected '57 Chevy, headed to our favorite beach on a beautiful Southern California summer's day while listening to our own song on the radio was just about as good as it could get. As soon as it was over, I changed the station to the number two rock station in LA, KRLA. Guess what song they were playing? Yes, "Baby Talk." We went crazy. As soon as it ended I changed the station again to KHJ, which was the up-and-coming number three station. Guess what? That's right. "Baby Talk" was right there. This did it. I was so excited I flipped over the front seat into the back seat. We were stoked!

When the song was over I climbed back into the front seat. For the rest of the ride we tried to figure out how I flipped over the seat. I tried to duplicate it, and I couldn't. Guess we will just have to wait until "Baby Talk" once again aligns itself on all three radio stations at the same time and see what happens.

✳ ✳ ✳

Arriving at the beach we immediately signed up for volleyball and settled in to play cards. Jan had a girlfriend who was usually at the beach. Her name was Jill Gibson. She was a beautiful, tall, thin blonde, but this particular day she was not there. Jan spotted an attractive high school girl he had recently met who was sitting with another attractive girl. He went and talked to them for a while. Upon returning to the card game Jan asked if I had noticed the girls he had been talking to. Then he proceeds to tell me that he had invited them up to his house after the beach. He went on to explain that they were Marymount students. The brunette was Ann Marshall and the blonde was Judy Lovejoy, daughter of the actor Frank Lovejoy. They were both very pretty girls, and I was looking forward to meeting them.

My old girlfriend, Cindy, had started to date one of our high school buddies. Cindy was very mature for her age and she wanted to get married and start raising kids. I think she could see that I was not a very good candidate for settling down. When the beach day was over, we headed for Jan's. Ann and Judy arrived shortly thereafter. We talked, laughed, and listened to some records. Judy and I were hitting it off really well so I asked her for her phone number. And she gave it to me. Wow! The daughter of a famous actor, and she who drove her own '57 T-Bird with a Continental kit. What a day. I called her later that night. She had her own phone! She invited me over to her house the following day.

I was really excited when I pulled up in front of her big, beautiful Beverly Hills home. Her white T-Bird was parked in the driveway. The lawn was a rich green, and there were a lot of trees. I took a deep breath and rang the doorbell.

Judy answered the door. She looked great. Most of her family was home. She introduced me to her mom, younger brother, and her grandmother who lived with them. She took me on a tour of the house. It was gorgeous. It started to cross my mind that maybe I was out of my league. Somehow the '32 Ford pickup truck parked in front of their Beverly Hills mansion was starting to seem very much out of place. Some of their neighbors included Doris Day and her husband Marty Melcher and their teenage son Terry as well as Danny Thomas and his family, and Lucille Ball and Desi Arnez and their kids. Judy's dad was at a business meeting and would not be back until later that evening. I was then invited to a family dinner the following night.

I was very nervous as I arrived for that dinner the next day. Everyone was already seated at the large dining room table. I was introduced to Mr. Lovejoy, who was sitting at the head of the table. We shook hands and he gave me a friendly smile and I sat down next to Judy. The china was exquisite and the silverware was magnificent, and I'm trying to remember which fork is for the salad. Shit, to this day I'm still not sure. The door to the kitchen swung open, and a servant started bringing in the dinner. Holy shit! One of the family members didn't make dinner? I was blown away.

After we had finished the main course, the same person showed up right on cue to pick up the dishes. Then when we decided it was time for desert the person serving us showed up again right on cue. Did they have ESP? After dessert Frank took after-dinner drink requests. Then I noticed that he pushed a little button on the side of the table and out popped the servant. Now that is really cool, I thought. We talked and laughed as we enjoyed our after dinner drinks. Frank seemed like a really nice man. Then Judy said, "Let's go for a ride in the T-Bird!"

It was a beautiful night to go for a ride. We drove west on Sunset towards the beach, turned onto Pacific Coast Highway, and then into a driveway that led to a parking lot. We parked in front of a large building that I had seen many times before but never known much about. Judy smiled and announced that she has the keys.

"The keys to what?" I wanted to know.

"The keys to the cabana!"

"What cabana?"

"We belong to the Beach Club and we have our own private beach cabana." Holy shit! This is like knowing a girl with her own apartment! I didn't know any girls with their own apartments.

None of my friends knew any girls with their own apartments, they were all still living at home with their parents or in a dorm. The closest Cindy and I got to our own private space, besides the typical front or backseat of the car, was to sneak into the family garage, and climb into her mom's four-door passenger car for an intimate make out session. Now I was looking at a cabana, right on the beach, with its own bathroom, bar, and sound system. Thank you Lord, I have indeed died and gone to heaven!

After some heavy making out, we realized that it was getting late and decided to head home. On the drive back to Beverly Hills, I tell her, in a roundabout way, how overwhelmed I feel by her house, servants, sports car, famous father, and beach club private cabana. She looks me right in the eye and says, "My Dad hasn't worked in more than two years. He wants to get rid of the cabana and give up the membership to the Beach Club, but Mom won't let him. He has had to sell off some investments to pay the bills." I was shocked. This was my first major lesson on what a difference there could be between appearances and reality. Welcome to the world of smoke and mirrors. Well, one thing was for sure—Judy was one great kisser!

Meanwhile, believe it or not, even though we had a hit record on the radio (at least in LA), we still had never performed live in front of an audience. Lou informed us one day that he had booked us at "Teen Night at Nu-Pike" in Long Beach on June 25, a Thursday night. Now was the "moment of truth" for me. Jan had already performed live and was a natural at it. I was still coming to terms with the fact that, at least for the moment, we really had a hit record and everything was taking off a lot quicker than I had anticipated. I was nervous about performing live.

The big day came and Lou drove us to the Nu-Pike Fun Park. I was feeling incredibly nervous as we drove to the park. I really didn't like feeling this way at all. This should have been exciting and I was dreading it. Is this "stage fright"? I wondered. Because if it is, I don't want any part of it. Could this have been Arnie's problem with the entertainment business? If it was I didn't blame him for getting out.

We finally got to the park. We were led to our dressing room and I went straight to the bathroom and threw up. The rest of the night was a blur. Everyone said that we put on a really good show, but I don't remember any of it—except for the throwing up part. On the ride home I worried about what I would feel like the next time we played live. If the anxiety continued, I didn't know if I could keep doing it.

Over the next couple of days we were waiting to find out if we had taken a significant jump up on both the KFWB Top 40 chart and the Music City chart. If we managed to move up on the charts, we could send them to Dick Clark and possibly get booked onto *American Bandstand*. Oh, God! I was now faced with the realization that we were really going to perform on a show, and not just any show, but on *American Bandstand*! I really had thought that this would never happen. And I was starting to realize that I wasn't really prepared for any of this. Was that normal?

The realization that we were really going to have to get on a plane and fly to the East Coast, where I had never been, show up at the WFIL-TV station, walk into the *American Bandstand* set, be introduced by the real, in the flesh Dick Clark, and sing our very own song, "Baby Talk," on national TV, made me light-headed and sick to my stomach.

The morning we left to fly to Philadelphia, Lou's wife Deanna gave Jan and me big, thick gold St. Christophers on beautiful gold chains for good luck and to protect us in our travels. They were obviously very expensive. I commented to Jan what a nice gift that was, but I wondered why she had spent all of that money on expensive jewelry—we would have been happy with a box of doughnuts. Jan said not to worry about the money since Deanna is independently wealthy. Wow, another piece of the puzzle had now been solved.

My first recollection of arriving in Philadelphia was that it was hot and humid. I had never been anywhere further east than Montana. What in the world was this kind of heat? And why was everything so dirty and crowded? What a disturbing place! But at the same time it was incredibly exciting.

After we had checked into our hotel, Lou, Jan, and I went to the hotel restaurant. When we get there, they won't let us in because we aren't wearing jackets. But we were too hungry to go elsewhere, so the maître d' agrees to loan us some. The jackets are hideous and stink of old cigars, but we're so hungry we don't care. When the food finally comes it's so greasy it's almost inedible—but we eat it anyway. Well, at least they can't screw up the ice cream, can they? It turns out that they could! It was mushy and had dirt in it. What a weird place this is! Actually, the vanilla ice cream was vanilla bean—it was supposed to have little black specks in it, or so we were to find out later.

The next day we were picked up by our promotion man and driven to the WFIL-TV station. It was under some train tracks and pretty dark and dingy. Once inside we are taken into Dick Clark's office. He is just finishing up a meeting. When he sees Jan he seems to be genuinely happy to see him. Then he is introduced to me. While I am very much in awe, I am also acutely aware that this is one genuinely nice person.

Back in our dressing room we practice our routine. I'm nervous again, but not as much as before. They call us to the set a few minutes later. Dick introduces us to the *Bandstand* audience, we sing our song, and in a blink it's over. The song is only two minutes and seventeen seconds long. Wow, that was fun! The chicks screamed. It was wild! We were put into the autograph booth where we spent the rest of the show, signing autographs. I had to ask Jan what I should write—I had just realized that I had never signed an autograph before. Jan suggested that we just write "Best Wishes" and our first names.

After the show we were invited to Pop's Soda Fountain to hang out with the Bandstand staff and the Bandstand dancers. The jukebox was playing Dion and the Belmonts, Freddy Cannon, and Frankie Avalon. I hoped "Baby Talk" would be big enough to make it onto that jukebox someday. That would be really, really cool!

The next day it's hot and muggy. Our promo man picks us up and takes us to some of the radio stations in town. He may have been old, fat, and dressed in wrinkled, baggy clothes, but he was a really nice man and an old pro. He knew everybody in the region that could make things happen. When we got in his car we saw what a mess it was. It was rusty and dirty and the trunk was packed with boxes of newly pressed 45s. The smell of vinyl was almost overwhelming. We drove from station to station dropping off records and meeting program directors and DJs. The streets were crowded with people, bicycles, cars, and more taxis than I had ever seen in my life. And the horns! Everybody that had one used it—a lot! I tried to recall the last time I used my horn. I think it was Christmas Day, 1957.

The promo man said he needed to drop by the record pressing plant to pick up more records. Did we want to check it out? Sure. We had never seen records being pressed before. The building was very old and made of brick. There were large skylights and most of the glass panels were cracked or missing altogether. There must have been at least a hundred record pressing machines chugging away. They kind of looked like greasy, giant waffle irons.

Then we found a couple of machines making our record. That was really a thrill! We also noticed a bunch of machines that were pressing a song by Skip & Flip called "It Was I," one of our favorite songs. There were also some machines pressing the new Freddy Cannon record. Wow! All of these records were songs being played heavily on *American Bandstand*. It was obvious to me that all those plays on *American Bandstand* kept these presses really busy. I commented that the Mallory family, who owns the pressing plant, must be very thankful to Dick Clark. The promo man gave me a squinty look.

"The Mallory family doesn't own this pressing plant, Dick Clark does. Mallory is his wife's maiden name," he says. Holy shit! Another lesson; nothing is left to chance. There are reasons for everything. I'd better start paying a lot more attention to all the things going on around me.

Over the next few days, "Baby Talk" national sales were starting to take off. It looked like it was going to be a legitimate national hit. Dick Clark invited us to perform "Baby Talk" on his Saturday night show. Only proven hits were performed on the Saturday night show. Man, we really were for real! We had only planned to stay for one week, but we got a call from Dick Clark's office asking if we could stay an extra couple of days and perform on the Saturday night show again. Wow, two Saturday nights in a row. A group that was supposed to play broke up and had cancelled at the last minute, and since we had one of the hottest new records, they thought we would be a great replacement.

We couldn't believe it! One performance on the Saturday night show could easily generate at least 150,000 record sales and a jump of maybe 20 to 30 chart positions. And Dick Clark thinks we're doing *him* a favor? We were bouncing off our hotel room walls. When we showed up for the show we found two beautiful fruit baskets, a couple of cases of Spearmint chewing gum, and a handwritten note from Dick Clark saying, "Thank you for pulling the chestnuts out of the fire." I still have that note in my scrapbook. It taught me to always pay attention to anyone who helps you accomplish a task—and that we were all in this together. We needed him, he needed us, and everyone on the team needed to be acknowledged as contributing to the final product, no matter how minor a contribution it was.

Arriving back home we were totally amazed at the profound difference in our lives. Having done three Dick Clark performances in a little over two weeks had put us in an entirely different universe! Lou called me a couple of days after we had gotten home.

"Guess where the record went on the KFWB and Music City chart for next week?" he asked.

"I don't know, just tell me," I said.

"Number one," he responded proudly. To this day I remember exactly how I felt at that moment, because for the longest time I couldn't figure out why I said what I said.

"Oh no, Lou, it's moving too fast."

Lou was stunned. He of course expected me to be thrilled—but I wasn't.

It took a couple of days until I was able to articulate my feelings. Yes, having a number one record was extremely special, to be sure, but number one is as high as you can go. So guess what happens next. That's right, it goes back the same direction it came from—back to zero. It's over. It's had its run. It's an oldie. The party is over, so are you ready with the follow-up? What follow-up? Shit! In eight weeks we went from unknowns to number one! I wanted this feeling to last a while. It didn't seem fair. Just eight weeks—I had zits that lasted longer than that. I was acutely aware of what the odds were to have one hit record in the first place, and I was equally aware of how those odds would be geometrically compounded by trying to record a second hit record.

But now for the good news. Nationally we were five to six weeks behind the Los Angeles market, so we were able to have more time to enjoy our climb up the national charts. Unfortunately, by having a record that already peaked in a major market like Los Angeles, by the time we were number one elsewhere, with all of the LA sales over, this would probably keep us from having the number one record in the country. "Baby Talk" finally did peak at number ten on September 14, 1959. Hey, not bad, not bad at all.

3
THE BEACH BOYS

{1962–1963}

One early spring day in 1962, Jan and I were driving to the beach in my newly custom painted, fuel-injected Corvette. I had spent months hand-sanding the fiberglass. I had taken off all the chrome. The guy from the Japanese body shop I frequented painted the car with twenty coats of Chinese red lacquer. The indent on the side of the car that was normally painted white at the factory, I had painted jet black. I removed the fake knock-off hubcaps, painted the rims jet black, and put on small, button Chevy hubcaps. For Christmas my now girlfriend Judy had bought me a beautiful handcrafted wooden Nardi steering wheel made in Italy, and she had my name engraved on one of the polished aluminum spokes. Jan & Dean were two cool cats!

The radio was always on KFWB. One day all of a sudden this record comes on . . . "Surfin' is the only way, the only life for me, so come on pretty baby and surf with me, yeah, bomp bomp dipadittydip bomp bomp dipadittydip." We looked at each other, our jaws wide open. Who the hell are these guys, and why have they stolen our bomps and they even had the gall to swipe our dipadittydips just to really rub it in! And why the heck are they singing about surfin'?

We listened intently, and at the end of the record the DJ said, "That's 'Surfin'" by The Beach Boys." The Beach Boys! What a great name! But still, a song about surfing? Why would anyone care? We could count on one hand all of our friends who surfed. On a big day at Malibu there might be fifty guys. How many surfers could there be in California? A couple thousand? At most? Where else do they surf? Not that many places, to be sure. Does anybody care about music about surfing besides surfers? These were interesting questions to be sure. We decided we had better keep our eye on this record.

Over the next few days we heard "Surfin'" a lot. We called Lou to see what he knew about the record. He said it was on a small independent record label called Candex. The record seemed to be just more of a regional hit. It was on the national charts but just barely. Well, I guess that answers the question, "Does anybody inland care about a record about surfing?" I guess not.

We were struggling with our own career problems at the time. It had been a year since our remake of the hit "Heart and Soul." We needed to retool our style. Up to this point we were a typical duo: two vocals with some occasional female background singers. Status quo. We had just changed labels again, for the fourth time. The new company was a very successful independent company. The first record with each of our previous labels had always turned out to be a big hit, but not this time. The record company tried everything. They asked Lou to step aside and let their hotshot young record producer Snuff Garrett have a shot at getting Jan & Dean a hit. That didn't work either. Then they got so desperate they put the record company's president's kid in charge of helping us record a hit. Now Lenny Waronker was showing early signs of talent to be sure, but he was sixteen years old for God's sake. His mom had to drive him to the studio. That didn't work out so well either.

Nobody at the company had any new ideas so they did what they usually did best—resort back to old ideas. Hey, let's put together a golden hits album, they said. Never mind that. Jan & Dean don't have enough hits to do a golden hits album. Well, said the record company executives, we never really said whose golden hits we are talking about did we? So they bought the rights to some of those past Jan & Dean hits from the other three record labels. Then they tried to talk us into supplementing the rest of the album with Jan & Dean's versions of other people's golden hits. Hey, who will know the difference? Wink, wink.

For lack of anything better to do, we agreed to give it a try. We thought maybe this would give us the opportunity to experiment with other people's styles. Recording studios were starting to realize that pop music was here to stay and that new young recording artists were going to start pushing the envelope, and they were all going to have to keep up with all of the new advanced recording technologies. So the time was right for experimentation.

We got a lot of inspiration listening to the new group The Four Seasons. Their hit record, "Sherry," was one great record. The lead vocal was all in falsetto and the background parts were strong masculine four-part harmonies. Our trademark had been to use falsetto only at the end of a record. Maybe we should try doing a Four Seasons song on our golden hits album? And maybe look for another falsetto lead song as well? Maybe that old song, "Barbara Ann" by the Regents would work. That would be perfect—with the more advanced recording techniques now at our fingertips, we could sing all of the background harmony parts ourselves. The advantage to this was that you would have all the same vocal tones and phrasing. This could be a really cool sound for us.

So in the studio we started experimenting with doubling vocal parts by singing in unison to a vocal part previously recorded. This made a vocal part seem fatter, almost choir-like. We started doubling the four-part harmonies, then the lead vocals—espe-cially the falsettos. We knew we were onto something. When we finished the golden hits album, we knew there were a few clunk-ers on it that we did for the benefit of Lou's new company. But we loved "Barbara Ann." We asked the record company geniuses to put "Barbara Ann" out as a single. It was the oldest remake on the album—at least four years old by that time. Nothing else made any sense as a single. But the shitheads running the record company concluded that the song "Barbara Ann" was way too primitive and could never be a hit again. Never! Never? Hmmm.

We decided that the "Barbara Ann" formula was a sound one. So now we started looking for a song about a girl that used a girl's name in the title. Since 60 percent of rock-and-roll record buyers were teenage girls, it seemed like a good idea. Then we would sing all the lead vocals in falsetto, add lots of four-part harmonies, and throw some doo-wops in for good measure.

A friend suggested an old fifties song, "Linda." Wow, this song fulfilled all the criteria, it was perfect. We recorded it using all our new recording techniques. The finished "Linda" recording was a breakthrough for us. Yes, the lyrics were corny, but Jan's record production was spot on. We had made a quantum leap from our last hit record, "Heart and Soul." Our new record debuted on the national charts, February 23, 1963, at #90. It looked like we had another big hit brewing!

Then, Christ! Those surfin' guys were back again! Didn't they learn their lesson? Now they have a song out titled, "Surfin' Safari." But wait a minute, it's on a serious label—a very serious label—Capitol Records. The Beach Boys are no longer in the minor leagues. "Linda" and "Surfin' Safari" were all over the radio together. It was great.

* * *

For the most part, the majority of the hit records were still coming from the East Coast. So when a local LA concert promoter went looking for acts that had records on the charts, there were not that many choices. It was inevitable that a promoter would put Jan & Dean and The Beach Boys together. This pairing also saved the promoter some money. The promoter told The Beach Boys that if they wanted the gig, they would have to back up the headliners, Jan & Dean! They were told to learn the "vast" Jan & Dean set list, maybe ten songs. Five were Jan & Dean songs, five were the usual rock 'n' roll standards, and there was at least one Chuck Berry song, since we all liked Chuck Berry songs.

When we showed up at the high school where the concert was to be held, we were taken to a dressing room that we were sharing with The Beach Boys. We walked into the room not knowing what to expect. They were all there: Mike, Brian, Carl, Dennis, and David. They, too, didn't know what to expect. I mean, we were the old guys, already twenty years old, with two gold records, driving very cool, shiny new Corvettes.

We all shook hands and introduced ourselves. They were just kids, nice kids, but just kids all the same. We small talked, then got down to business. We needed to run through our music set and, as I remember, they were very-well prepared. We all got dressed and then they went on first.

They played for about half an hour, and then we were introduced. We did our ten songs, bowed, and walked off. Well the audience wanted more. We had not thought about an encore song. It hadn't even occurred to us to do so. So we thought maybe we could just stay off the stage and the audience would give up on an encore and go home. That didn't happen. They wouldn't stop. What the hell are we going to do now? I thought. We hadn't rehearsed any more songs with The Beach Boys. The promoter was having a meltdown. The show was short by at least ten minutes—a couple of songs worth. He forced us back on stage.

We walked back on and looked at one another as if to say, "Well, what the hell do we do now?" It would be very garage bandish to repeat a song you just did a few minutes ago. The Beach Boys were willing to do it, but we really were opposed to repeating any of our songs.

"Hey, I got an idea," I told them. "Let's do 'Surfin' and 'Surfin' Safari.'" Those were legitimate hits, not someone else's hits. It had been a while since those songs had been played. "Is that okay with you?" I asked Brian. They all looked stunned and pleased at the same time, and I actually was looking forward to singing their songs. Their songs were a lot of fun to sing, and Jan and I had really missed singing in a vocal group—this felt like being back on stage with The Barons.

We launched into the two surf songs, Jan and I adding two extra parts. It sounded sooooo cool. The audience loved it. From that moment on The Beach Boys could see we were team players, and we really respected everything they had accomplished. Afterward Jan and Brian exchanged phone numbers. Do I hear Humphrey Bogart's voice again?

A few weeks later we were given the green light to start a "Linda" titled album. We needed to come up with a concept. The "Baby Talk" album was kind of a girls' names album because the followup to the single, "Baby Talk," was titled "There's A Girl." We knew that the title to our new album would have to have the name of our latest hit single, "Linda" in it. Maybe we could record "Sherry" and we could even throw in "Barbara Ann." More girls' names could always work as a concept, but then again, in the long run we decided it was time to start to shed that teen idol crap. We had been there and done that—time to blow it up and start a reinvention of sorts, and we would start by burning our suits! Southern California lifestyle here we come.

The record company nitwits would go ballistic over this. Teen idol heartthrob shit was still the mainstay of the record business. Why would anybody want to tamper with this proven formula? Well, we were ready to tamper. We thought about doing some of those cool surf songs. They were really fun to sing. Only problem was that, to date, there were only two vocal songs written about surfing, and Brian Wilson had written both of them. We weren't really sure if Brian wanted us to record his songs. But the Beach Boys versions had already run their course, so we thought our versions wouldn't impact their sales at all.

Jan called Brian and told him our idea: "Jan & Dean Take Linda Surfing." That would accomplish two major goals: it would get the hit title "Linda" on the front of the album cover, but we would also get the word "surfing" on the cover as well. Plus, graphically we could start to explore visual beach themes—the sun, the sand, hot rod woodies, surfboards, ocean, palm trees, and yeah, Linda in a bathing suit. Now we're cooking.

Brian loved the idea. He said as a songwriter he would be flattered if Jan & Dean did their own versions of his "Surfin'" and "Surfin' Safari" songs—not to mention that he stood to make some extra royalty loot off of the pending sales from the new project. Jan recognized how stoked (that's an old surfing term) Brian sounded about the project, and decided to get even bolder. "Say, Brian, it sure would save us some time and money if you would consider coming into the recording studio and playing the instrumental tracks for us. And while you are there you could maybe help us with the vocals, just like we did on stage a couple of weeks ago." Brian agreed.

March 4, 1963, we were all in the studio together recording "Surfin'" and "Surfin' Safari." Jan and I loved it. We were finally back in a vocal band. It felt perfect.

Brian was astounded by Jan's technical knowledge, and Jan was enjoying sharing his information with Brian. Brian shared some of his vocal harmony expertise with us. Brian was more musically creative than Jan, but Jan was a brilliant technician. I, on the other hand, was less musically knowledgeable than Jan or Brian, but I was more conceptually creative, and I was almost always the one who interjected the humor into our projects. We all had different strengths, and this made for a pretty interesting team.

We had a blast recording with those guys. They, like us, were making music together because they enjoyed the process of creating music and making records. We weren't counting on getting rich, making movies, buying palatial estates, or riding around in limos and private jets. It was fun to develop a musical idea into a tangible project.

After we finished the two tunes, Brian sat down at the piano and asked us if we wanted to hear The Beach Boys' next single. Of course we did. "If everybody had an ocean across the USA, then everybody would be surfin' like Cala-forn-i-a." Ahhh, excuse me, Brian, that is a great song, but the melody sounds exactly like "Sweet Little Sixteen" by Chuck Berry. Jan told Brian that he would get in big trouble when Chuck Berry heard the song. "Sweet Little Sixteen" was copyrighted, both the melody and the lyrics, so you couldn't just take the melody and change the words. It doesn't work that way.

Jan suggested that Brian should give us "Surfin' USA" because we know Chuck, and Jan was sure that he could work it out somehow. Brian said his dad didn't think there would be a problem so he wasn't worried about it.

"But, you know, I do have this other surf song that's similar. I will probably do only one or the other and 'Surfin' USA' is my favorite. So if you want, you can have the other one. You'll have to finish it. Want to hear it?"

"Sure."

"Okay, I'll sing it to you."

So he sits back down at the piano and starts to play:

Two girls for every boy.
I bought a '33 panel truck and I call it my woody.
It's not very cherry, it's an oldie but a goodie.
It ain't got a heater or a radio,
but it still gets me where I wanna go.

"Well, that's the first verse, what do you think?"

"Wow! We'll take it. What's it called?"

"Surf City."

"It's a deal."

"The song is yours—change it any way you want to."

"Thank you so much, Brian. So what else do you have that you've lost interest in?"

"Well, I do have this other song called 'When Summer Comes Gonna Hustle You.'" He plays it.

"Damn, that's a great song, too. We'll take that one too if you don't mind!"

Jan went right to work on the arrangements for the instrumental tracks. He was really pleased with the chemistry of the new studio musicians he had handpicked. Hal Blaine was on drums, Ray Pulman on bass, Leon Russell on keyboards, Glen Campbell on lead guitar, and Tommy Tedesco on rhythm guitar. But Jan wanted to try something new. He wanted to hear what two drummers playing at the same time sounded like. So he added our old drummer, Earl Palmer, into the mix.

Jan would write out each and every part for each instrument, including the drums. So the two drummers set up their kits side by side and read off of identical charts. What a great sound! These tracks were the best that Jan had ever done. He had definitely arrived.

Jan had also formed a special relationship with an up-and-coming studio engineer, Bones Howe. This guy was not only a great recording engineer, but he was also extremely creative. Now with the instrumental tracks done, we were ready for the vocals. "When Summer Comes Gonna Hustle You" was lyrically complete, so we worked on that one first. Plus, it was a pre-summer, spring semester song, and "Surf City" was definitely a summer song. We loved, "Gonna Hustle You." It was the quintessential Brian Wilson musical story, full of fifties innocence, plus it was a doo-wopper.

When it was finished, we played it for the "suits" at the record company. They looked shocked.

"What's wrong?"

"You can't say 'hustle you' on the radio!"

"Say what? Run that by us again."

"You can't use the words 'hustle you' on the radio. Get rid of it!"

"We can't. It's in the goddamn title, you morons!"

"Well, delete it, change it to something else."

"'When Summer Comes, Gonna (Blank) You?' What kind of sense does that make?"

"Change the words! Maybe, 'When Summer Comes, Gonna Date You.'"

We about puked all over their shiny Continental suits!

"You can't be serious!"

"Dead serious! We will not put that record out if that word"—cover your ears folks—"'hustle' is still in it."

We were dumbfounded! What were these dimwits talking about? Is this a bad dream? A *Candid Camera* bit? A CIA experiment? We took our demo lacquer off the turntable and left. Damn it, this is the best record we had made to date and the assholes won't release it. What in the world is wrong with the word "hustle" anyway? We were thoroughly confused.

That evening, around the dinner table, I asked my dad what he thought about the word "hustle." He said that to his generation it was a suggestive word used as another way of saying "proposition." We had to remember that our parents were raised in the Victorian age. I wonder what they thought when they heard the Stones singing, "I can't get no satisfaction." It wasn't that far off in the future.

So we now focused on "Surf City." All we needed to do was to finish the lyrics and then the song was ready for the vocals.

Once in the studio, Jan, Brian, and I laid down the four-part harmony background vocals first, and then we doubled them. Then Jan did the low bass background part and doubled that. Then Brian and I did the falsetto parts and doubled those as well. What a great sound. Brian's falsetto was airy, smooth, angelic, and round sounding. Mine was a lot less airy—what they refer to as a head falsetto, less from the diaphragm and more from the sinus, sounding a lot more top end, trebly, and edgier than Brian's. Together, we had the full range of sounds. Our phrasing was noticeably different, causing almost a Doppler effect. There was a time when we would have kept doing it over and over and over until our phrasing matched. But now it was more fashionable to experiment and be more imaginative than musically correct. This was always hard for Jan to accept. But if Brian said it was okay, it was okay.

The more we listened to it we realized that this out of sync phrasing created some interesting harmonics, or what would later be called phasing by guitarists. Brian thought it was really cool. "Leave it alone, keep it as it is! Don't touch it!" Jan didn't.

Now it was time to sing the lead vocal. Brian wrote out the complete song combining Jan's contribution to the lyrics with his own old lyrics, then he showed it to me for my two cents. I imme-diately noticed the first line, "I bought a '33 panel truck and we call it a woody."

I said, "Brian, a panel truck is a metal paneled truck. It doesn't have wood on it. It doesn't have side windows. It's solid metal. It's a truck, not a station wagon." So I crossed out the words "panel truck" in my distinctive printing and I wrote the word "wagon." There, that's better.

"I bought a '33 wagon and we call it a woody." But then I started to wonder if they made station wagons in 1933.

"Brian, I don't think Ford made any cars in 1933, but I do know they did in 1932. That's what we now call a Deuce. But I don't recall seeing a Deuce station wagon, although I have seen a '34 station wagon. Okay to change '33 to '34?" It was okay with him.

"Also, Brian, you wrote 'it ain't got a heater or a radio.' Well, maybe we don't need a heater, but ya gotta have a radio. You've got to be able to listen to surf music in a car, don't ya? So if this woody is missing anything, it should be the back seat and the rear window, because that's where the surf boards go. Plus, window rhymes with 'go' in the next line. Check it out."

> *It ain't got a back seat, or a rear window,*
> *but it still gets me where I wanna go.*

Next, I noticed the line, "There's two swingin' girls for every guy, and all you got to do is just wink your eye."

"Brian, surfers call their girls 'honeys' don't they? Let's drop the word 'girl' and replace it with 'honeys.'"

> *There's two swingin' honeys for every guy,*
> *and all you got to do is just wink your eye.*

"How's that?"
He liked it.

"Let's record it"

Jan and Brian sang the lead vocal together, and then doubled it. It was meant for Brian's vocal to be just behind Jan's, shadowing it. This was intended just as some subtle support, but somehow by the time it was ready for the final mix, his vocals ended up being a lot more prominent than they were meant to be. But because he and Jan sang it together at the same time, and not on separate tracks, nothing could be done about it, without starting over. We didn't want to touch it. The final mix of the record came out great. This was by far the best Jan & Dean record we had ever made. The record was released May 17, 1963, and just flat took off.

A Capitol Records promotion man was driving in his car when he first heard "Surf City" on the radio. He pulled over, got on a pay phone, called Capitol Records' offices in Los Angeles, and demanded to know why he had not been given the new Beach Boys record to deliver to the radio stations himself. This was embarrassing. The new Beach Boys record was already on the radio and he didn't even know about it. Hey, what gives? Have I been fired? The "suits" at the record company were as confused as he was. There wasn't any new Beach Boys record out that they knew about. It was their understanding that it wasn't finished yet. So what's going on, the promotion man asked. The "suits" think maybe it might have been bootlegged or something. They tell the promo man to head on over to the radio station and find out how they got the record.

At the radio station, the promo man is informed that it was not a Beach Boys record he had heard, it was a Jan & Dean record, and it's a smash hit. He now calls back to corporate with the bad news. Somebody else has done a surf music record and it appears that it is going to be a monster hit, and yes, it does sound a lot like a Beach Boys record. He said he would ask to get a closer look at the record in hopes of gathering more information about it, and will report back ASAP.

He is finally handed the record. He notes that it is on Liberty Records, the artists are Jan & Dean, and the writers are Wilson and Berry. "Hey, wait a minute, isn't one of the Beach Boys named Wilson? Why would he cowrite a song for the competition?" The promo man asks to hear the record again. "Man it sounds more like The Beach Boys than any typical Jan & Dean recording. There is a voice that sounds a lot like a voice heard on the Beach Boys recordings."

The promo man calls back to corporate with the new information. Corporate goes nuts. They get right on the phone and call The Beach Boys' manager, Murray Wilson, father of three of the Beach Boys. Now Murray goes ballistic and calls Brian. Brian tries to explain to his dad that it was a song he was never going to finish, so why not get some use out of it? But Murray was out of control. He called us "record pirates" and forbids Brian to give us any more songs, forbids him to sing or play on any future Jan & Dean records, "and for that matter, don't associate with them anymore either. Period."

Brian was hurt and confused by his dad's irrational demands. Brian and his dad owned a music publishing company together, and in Brian's way of looking at it, "Surf City" was a song he had lost interest in. It probably would have never been a Beach Boys record and besides, Brian thought that "Surfin' USA" was a much better song. So, as a songwriter and music publisher, to have someone else record your leftovers and derive some royalties from those leftovers should be something to strive for, not to avoid. And the competition argument? Hey, there was plenty of room on the charts for everybody. Plus, this competition was friendly and beneficial to both parties.

Murray's distorted point of view and his lack of experience in the music industry was what eventually got him fired from the Beach Boys' team. The rest of The Beach Boys initially wished

Brian wouldn't have been quite so helpful, but as time passed, they realized that our musical connections were not only beneficial to each other, but enjoyable too. We were one of their biggest fans and I always felt the feeling was mutual. Some fifty plus years later they do some of our songs in their live concerts, including "Surf City," and we do a bunch of theirs in our live concerts as well.

June 1, *Billboard Magazine* makes "Surf City" the Spotlight Winner of the Week and a Billboard Pick, with a quote, "Two more swinging sides by the hot West Coast team." June 2, "Surf City" debuts at #7 on LA's KRLA radio station. Jan & Dean play with The Beach Boys in Modesto, California, on June 5, again on June 7 at Veterans Hall in Bakersfield, California, and again on June 8 in Palmdale, California.

June 16, "Surf City" is the number one song in the Los Angeles market. June 22, "Surf City" is the number one song in Florida and number twenty on The Billboard Chart and number twenty-eight on The Cashbox Chart and by June 29 we were in the top ten of both publications.

"Surf City" reached number one on both the Billboard and Cashbox Charts on July 27, 1963, replacing "Easier Said than Done" and just beating out "Fingertips" by Stevie Wonder. "Surf City" was the first surf song to reach number one. We were hot. There were TV offers, movie offers, and lots of concert offers. One of our favorite places to play was Hawaii. Tom Moffatt, a promoter and disc jockey based in Honolulu, loved putting Jan & Dean and The Beach Boys in concert together. These concerts were totally bitchin'! We had such a great time together. Because Brian had written a song called "Little Honda," the local Honda dealer in Waikiki gave us all free Honda Scramblers to ride while we were on the island.

Dennis Wilson and I would ride our Hondas from one end of the island to the other—even late at night, just like the song said, "Gonna turn on the light so I can ride my Honda tonight." We would often be shirtless riding in the topical rain in the moonlight, the warm wind blowing through our hair. The sweet smell of the ocean mixed with the intoxicating smell of plumeria and other tropical flowers. During the day, we would stop at all of our favorite body surfing beaches, especially at Makapu'u, breaking out a bottle of rum, then jumping into the warm Hawaiian surf. Later we would climb back on our Hondas and go balls out along Interstate H-1, past Chinaman's Hat, all the way up to Turtle Bay, then down to Sunset Beach, past Banzai Pipeline, past Waimea to Haleiwa, then cut over to Route 99 taking it all the way to Pearl Harbor, stopping just long enough to salute the USS *Arizona* memorial. We thought it was ironic, since we were riding Hondas. Then it was back to the Kahala Hilton and maybe a dip in the porpoise pool. Then we'd head to our rooms and fall asleep.

At one of our concerts, quite appropriately at Pearl Harbor, we all got in a huge fire extinguisher and shaving cream fight on stage. The music stopped for a good fifteen minutes. It was the first official battle of the surf bands. Brian's wife, Marilyn, and her sister Diane were there, and they documented the battle on their 8 mm black-and-white camera. To this day we are still looking for that piece of film. If you have it, advertise it on eBay. It's worth some righteous bucks.

At another concert, Jan had gotten into a fight with his girlfriend, Jill, at our hotel. He lost track of time and missed one of our matinee shows altogether. My Beach Boy pals helped me out by accompanying me on stage. The audience loved it, and so did I. Some nights we would all get together, order a couple rounds of every tropical drink the bar could make, then play Monopoly—with real money, of course. Or we'd play that old detective board game

Clue. We would often call friends back on the mainland to participate in the game with us over the phone. Obviously our phone bills
were outrageous, but we were rock stars. The game was over when
someone threw up or passed out. These were great times.

On one of these late-night flights home from Hawaii, Dennis
Wilson and I had brought a big bottle of rum on the plane. We were
celebrating the amazing time we had just had in Hawaii, and we
were toasting the Islands, each and every one. Then we toasted all
of our favorite surfing spots, each and every one. Then we toasted
all of our favorite Hawaii girlfriends. Uh-oh, there was some overlap. We settled in to our seats for the long ride back to the mainland. Sometime after we had been underway for a while, we found
ourselves lying on the floor by the door. We were eccentric, drunk
rock 'n' roll stars flying first class so nobody bothered us. And we
were having the time of our lives.

Somewhere in our ramblings, Dennis said that he had heard
through some anonymous snitch that Jan & Dean had tried to rip-
off a small-time concert promoter and what was that all about?

"Was it true? Who was the guy? Why and how did you do it?
But it's just really a bullshit story anyway, right?"

"Wrong," I told him. The rum was acting like sodium pento-
thal. "It's a true story, not bullshit at all." Dennis was surprised.
He was just sure that it was some made-up good old rock 'n' roll
folklore BS. It was a shock to him that somebody else could pull
off something even more outrageous than he was capable of. He
needed to know the whole story and, besides, it's a long flight.

It was Christmas 1961 or '62, so Jan and I had two weeks off
from school. Lou, our manager, had gotten a really good offer for
a nine-day concert tour through the Midwest playing mostly
ballrooms. The two other acts on the bill were Dick and Deedee,
whose "Mountain's High" was way up on the charts at this particular time. Also on the bill was a guy named Jerry Fuller, who

had a couple of chart records, but his real claim to fame was that he had written Ricky Nelson's current smash hit, "Travelin' Man." Well, it sounded like fun, so we agreed to be the headliners and do the tour.

The promoter sent us a 25 percent advance deposit. We were to be paid $500 a night, so for nine nights it would be a total of $4,500. The deposit of $1,100 had already been paid, so at the end of the tour the guy would owe us $3,400. Pretty righteous bucks for those days. A new Corvette was about $3,000. So we flew to Minneapolis on Thursday and stayed overnight. We were to meet the promoter in the lobby the next morning and then be driven to the first concert venue that night. We would drive to all nine venues, then be driven to Chicago to catch our flight home.

We showed up in the lobby the next morning where we met up with Dick and Deedee and Jerry Fuller. As we wait, we are approached by a short, weaselly looking man with a Howard Hughes pencil mustache wearing a long baggy trench coat and a stained forties style hat.

"What the fuck kind of stains?" Dennis wanted to know.

"I don't know, Dennis, why do you care?"

The guy comes up to us and introduces himself as TJ or TC Scarnning and asks if we are ready to go. Well, not much of a conversationalist.

We pick up our luggage and head out looking for the tour bus. We look around. We don't see any tour bus. TJ or TC has now opened the trunk of a late fifties four-door Ford. Well, maybe we are driving to the tour bus. Six people in a passenger car for a short ride to the bus isn't so bad.

"So how far away is the bus, TC or TJ?" He didn't answer. He must be hard of hearing, probably have to speak up. "So TC or TJ, where exactly is the bus?"

"What bus?" he responds.

"Uh, the one we are going to ride in with the backup band for the next nine days. That's the bus we are talking about." TC-TJ says the band has their own car with a trailer and there is no tour bus.

We all look at each other realizing that the six of us are going to drive around in this stinky old car for the next nine days. Jan says that when we stop for lunch he will call Lou and find out if the contract specified what the mode of transportation was supposed to be. We drove, and we drove, and we drove, and we drove. TC or TJ was not very talkative so we talked to one another pretty much nonstop.

By that time we were getting pretty hungry, so we asked him to stop so we could eat. He dropped us off at a café and said he would be back in an hour. What a strange little man, we thought. Plus we wondered where he was going and if he was coming back. Jan got right on the phone to Lou back in LA. Lou looked over the contract, but nowhere did it specify what the mode of transportation was to be provided. We had just assumed it would be a bus, but because it wasn't spelled out in the contract that Lou had signed, TC or TJ was not in violation of the contract. We were stuck.

Jan told us the bad news while we ate our lunch and waited for TC or TJ to pick us up. That night we met up with the backup band. They were really nice guys and easy to work with. We did a rehearsal with them and soon after that we played the first of nine concerts. It was a good show, relatively speaking, and very well attended. TC or TJ would go straight to the ticket booth. His deal was he had rented each ballroom for that particular night. This is called "four-walling." He would sit in the ticket booth himself selling each and every ticket. At the end of the evening he would pay the auditorium or ballroom manager and put the balance of the cash in his briefcase. After the concert we would change back into our traveling clothes, take our suitcases out to the car, put them in the trunk, and off we would go.

So we would drive for a while and then stop at a motel. The next morning we would get up and hit the road again. The next two weekend nights went very well. Monday morning we hit the road about lunchtime. Then we eventually pull into some small town and TC or TJ drops us off at a café as usual. We were still wondering where he would go each time he would drop us off. So Jan went outside to see where he went.

"I know," said Dennis, "he was fuckin' Deedee."

"Dennis, she was with us."

"Oh, okay, go on."

Jan saw TC or TJ go into a bank. He was probably getting rid of the cash and getting a cashier's check or something like that. It wasn't safe to carry around all that cash in his briefcase. That Monday night, and the next three nights were pretty much stiffs. TC-TJ looked very worried. Jan and I also started to worry. We were starting to get very concerned about the likelihood of us not getting paid. Jan called Lou. Lou said he had done some checking up on Mr. Scarnning and he had found out that Mr. Scarnning had just gotten out of prison.

Oh, fuckin' great! We have been driving for seven days in this ex-con's shitty car and we have three more days to go. We needed to take action. But what action?

"Let's ask him for our money in advance and if he says no we beat the shit out of the little weasel."

"No, that's probably not going to work. He will just remind us that the contract says 'upon completion of the tour we receive the balance due.'"

Another big problem—the contract didn't spell out in what form the balance was to be paid. It should have demanded we were to be paid in cash or a cashier's check or money order, not a company or personal check. We were fucked!

"This little weasel, sure as shit, is going to write us a worthless check and there is nothing we can do about it."

"Oh, yes, there is. Let's rob the little motherfucker."

"Um, he would probably recognize us."

"Let's hire some guys to rob him."

"No, they would probably double-cross us and keep the loot." Dennis's eyes were getting big. This was right up his alley.

"Hey, you know what we could do? We could steal his briefcase with all the cash in it."

"Whoa. That's a brilliant idea!"

The next three days were Friday, Saturday, and Sunday. He wouldn't be able to get to a bank until Monday, so by Sunday night there would be three nights of gross receipts. Let's see, an average of 650 people a night, at $4.50, would be almost $3,000 per night, times 3 nights—almost $9,000! Yeah, that's more like it. We had noticed that he usually kept the briefcase with him in the ticket booth. Then sometime towards the end of the concert he would settle up with the ballroom manager before taking the briefcase out to the car and locking it in the trunk. Then he would come back to the concert and try to make a move on any woman who looked like she'd be impressed that he was the boss. He could even arrange for them to get backstage to meet the stars, and gee, maybe he could make them stars someday too. After all, he did kinda look like Howard Hughes.

So the briefcase would be out in the trunk of the car all by itself until we arrived back at the motel. Then he would open up the trunk, take out the briefcase, and take it to his room. It was obvious the window of opportunity was when the briefcase was in the trunk of the car out in the ballroom parking lot. Our dressing rooms were usually right off the parking lot, and our car was usually very close to the stage door for load-in. The band's car and trailer were also close to that door so that we could unload and load up more quickly. The stage door was locked from the inside, so we could go out if needed and just keep it ajar so we could get back in. All we would need is a big screwdriver or a small crowbar to pop the trunk. It would be easy. Operation "Pop Goes the Weasel's Trunk" was officially in the works.

That Friday night we paid close attention to Mr. Scarnning, and like clockwork he followed the same routine. We practiced going in and out of the stage door, timing how long it took to go to the car, simulated popping the trunk, taking the briefcase out, and slamming the trunk shut, and then returning to the dressing room. We realized that coming into the well-lit dressing room area carrying a black briefcase posed a problem. Hey, take a suit bag out to the car, put the briefcase into the suit bag and walk back into the dressing room area. An entertainer returning from the band trailer with a suit bag would certainly look reasonable. No problem. Dick and Deedee would be on stage with the band. Jerry Fuller would be out working the crowd. It was usually just the two of us, maybe a janitor or maintenance person, but you could usually tell him it was time to get ready for our show and they would leave. Man, you know, this could really work out.

Sunday night became the target night. Dennis was intrigued. "Keep going." Saturday, at our lunch stop, we ate quickly then found a hardware store. We bought a claw crowbar, probably intended for pulling out nails. We rolled a sweater around it and headed back to the car. That Saturday night went well, and our little ex-con did pretty much his regular routine. We could easily have done it on that Saturday night, but we really wanted one more night of receipts.

All the next day we were all hyped-up with excitement. We couldn't wait to see the venue and get a fix on the layout. It was not much different than most of the other ballrooms. As a matter of fact, the stage door off the parking lot was one of the worst lit of the eight others. It also led to one of the darkest hallways we had experienced, absolutely perfect. There were multiple dressing rooms so we all had our own. We picked the one closest to the stage door. We timed practice runs from our dressing room, out the stage door to the car, allowing for some extra time popping the trunk, then locating the briefcase in the dark, putting it in a suit bag, coming back through the stage door, walking twenty feet to our dressing room, walking in, and closing the door. We were able to do this every time in a little over a minute or so. We also found a great place to ditch the briefcase.

The show finally got underway. The band did a couple of warm-up songs, and then Jerry did his songs. Now it was time for Dick and Deedee to do their show. We heard Dick and Deedee leave their dressing room and head for the stage. The clock was running. Jan grabs a suit bag with the crowbar in it and we open the dressing room door. The coast was clear. We opened the stage door and looked to see that nobody was lingering around in the parking lot. I stayed at the door as a lookout. Jan went out to the car. I heard a whomp noise and eight or nine seconds later Jan shows up at the door with a big smile.

We walked quickly back to our dressing room, closed the door, and locked it. We took the briefcase out of the suit bag, opened it, took out the money, which was in envelopes, put the money into one of our suitcases, and hid it under some clothes. We then took the empty briefcase and crowbar and threw it up through a hole in the ceiling that led to the attic. Then we replaced the cover. "Holy shit! We did it!" We laughed and high-fived. We could hardly believe it. We closed up our bags and headed for the stage. Since the trunk to the car still closed, we knew Mr. Scarnning wouldn't discover it was gone until later that evening. Dick and Deedee walked off and we walked on. We couldn't wait to get out of there, get to the motel, and count our money.

We finished our set and quickly returned to our dressing room to check on our loot. Ah, still there. We changed, then carried our bags out to the trailer. We piled into the car and headed to the motel. At the motel, TC or TJ told us to be ready to leave early the next morning and he would drive us to the airport. Then he handed us our checks. We had gotten our bags out of the trailer so we quickly went to our room. We popped open the bags with the money, excitedly opened the envelopes, and started counting.

Dennis was drooling. "How much? How much?" We had a little over $11,000. We were flipping out. We had scored big time. But then we started feeling sorry for Jerry, Dick, and Deedee. But, hey, they hadn't even given their final payment a second thought. We had anticipated a problem and taken action. We deserved the spoils.

Then we started to wonder what form of payment we had received. So we opened the envelope with the check. It wasn't a cashier's check or a money order. It was a company check. Some name we had never heard of. We then decided that if he was an honest man, in the morning when he picked us up, he would tell us that he had been ripped off and that because of that our checks were going to bounce, but he was pretty sure he had insurance and he would do whatever it took to make us whole. So we decided that if he told us the truth, we would tell him the truth, break out the cash, and divvy it up. But we were betting that wouldn't happen.

The next morning we all met at the car. TC or TJ was even quieter than usual. We piled into the car and he drove us to the airport. He didn't say a word. He dropped us off and drove away. We all watched him disappear into the gloomy morning mist, and shook our heads saying, "What a strange little man."

We were all on different flights, so we said our good-byes and good luck and Jan and I boarded our flight back to LA. Once we got seated, Jan opened up the carry-on bag and pulled out the envelopes of cash and we divided it up. Then we played one of our favorite games, Liar's Poker using the serial numbers of our heisted money. I won an extra $100 or $200 on the flight home. Back in LA we deposited the check and a few days later we were notified that it had bounced.

"What an asshole!" Dennis cried. But hold on Dennis—this is the best part of "Operation Pop Goes the Weasel's Trunk."

Now comes "Operation Pop Goes the Weasel's Trunk II." We took the bounced check straight over to our agent at the William Morris Agency and threw a shit fit. How could they allow us to get into this situation? Why didn't they get a much bigger deposit from Mr. Scarnning, especially when they had never worked with him before? And why didn't they do their due diligence before we left on tour. If we had known that he was an ex-con we would have stayed home. They didn't have a good answer, or at least one that we understood. We demanded the full deposit. No commissions taken out. No commissions on any future dates until we had recouped the full amount of the bounced check. They agreed. We also demanded a minimum of a 50 percent deposit on future dates, and the balance to be paid in cash before we went on stage. Period. They agreed. Then we stomped out, quickly heading for an outside corridor so we could finally break out laughing.

"And Dennis, one more kicker, the heisted cash was tax-free." Dennis was rolling on the floor belly laughing.

"Hey, let's drink a toast to Operation Pop Goes the Weasel's Trunk I and II!" We broke out the rum. The wheels were now turning—or more like wobbling. We both arrived at the same idea at the same time.

"Hey, what if we pulled off a new updated version of Operation Weasel?"

"Holy shit! Can you imagine the kind of cash we could get our hands on nowadays? We're not talking ballrooms—now we're talking about sports arenas, convention centers, even stadiums!"

"Hey, let's run some numbers. I'll get a pencil. We can write on this barf bag—well, unless you think you may need it. So let's see. The last place we played was an 11,000 seater. The ticket price was $8 so that's $88,000. They charged $1 for parking, so add at least another $5,000. Throw in food concessions and merchandize sales, probably another $15,000 to $20,000, and we are looking at more than $100,000 cash!"

"Hey, but if we waited to rip off a stadium you could quadruple that amount. So let's take a long hard look at our upcoming concert schedules and see if there may be a prime situation to consider as our new operation. Let's call it Operation Goofy Foot" ("goofy foot" being a left-footed surfer).

"Yeah, let's get together next week." We toasted Operation Goofy Foot and fell asleep on the floor.

Ok, I have to admit, I had too much to drink and I did embellish the story just a little bit. I mean, I am telling a story to Dennis Wilson, I had to make it really outrageous to keep his interest. Now it is true that Jan and I did plan the heist and intended to go through with the plan, but when we opened the backstage door leading out to the parking lot and out to the car, there was a security guy having a smoke just outside the door so we chickened out and went back to our dressing room. And by the way, Mr. Scarnning's check didn't bounce, and we were never able to verify that he was an ex-con. But he did resemble one, you know, the ones you saw in those black-and-white movies. Please don't tell Dennis.

4
ELVIS SIGHTING

{1964}

Jan and I had two high school buddies who were also in The Barons—not our singing group but in the YMCA sponsored Barons Club—who kidnapped Frank Sinatra Jr. Both Jan and I were called as witnesses in the kidnapping trial. It's a long story, but, one of the guys is writing a book about it. Anyone who wants to, can check it out when the book gets published.

On February 23, 1964, Jan and I were in court to testify as witnesses. Jan was called to the witness stand first. It was now already late in the day. After he testified, the court adjourned, and I was told to come back the following day. We had a concert to do in Hawaii, so Jan left for Hawaii the day I was to testify. The day after my trial appearance I flew to Hawaii. When my flight finally broke through the clouds, I caught my first sight of the island of Oahu. It always gave me goose bumps, the emerald green of the island framed by the brilliant blue of the Pacific Ocean. I love seeing Waikiki out the airplane window. I would always get a window seat on the left side of the plane, both coming and going. You could see the pink Royal Hawaiian Hotel, Diamond Head, Pearl Harbor, Honolulu, and sometimes even my favorite body surfing beach, Makapu'u. I also tried to find my old friend Tom Moffatt's house just off of Pali Highway.

The plane does a lazy turn and heads in. Once on the ground, the door opens and I swear you can smell the plumeria and hibiscus. What a great place! I looked at my watch and recalled that yesterday, at just about this exact time, I was on the stand sweating bullets. What a difference a day makes.

I took the short cab ride to the Eleki Hotel overlooking Waikiki. I went straight to my room on the fifth floor and opened up all the sliding glass windows to let in the tropical breezes. My telephone rings. It's our drummer, Hal Blaine. He wants to stop by and say hello. I was standing on the veranda, looking out over the beach when he arrived. He groped for words, unsure if he should even acknowledge any of the trial news. He finally said something like, "What a beautiful place this is. Everywhere you look there is beauty."

I told Hal that he was right and to come out on the veranda because I wanted to show him something really beautiful. He joined me on the veranda. I told him to look straight down. I said, "See the awning directly below us? Now can you see the back end of an armored Brink's truck?" He said he did. I told him that the last time I had stayed there I had noticed that the armored truck came and parked in that same spot at the same time every day. So I asked him if maybe, over the next few days, he could help me devise a plan where we could place ourselves on the awning and when the back door of the truck opened, we could swing in from above and rob that sucker clean. He about choked. I started laughing. He sighed in relief. "Oh, thank God. I thought you were serious!" Well, then again, Hal, maybe I was.

After lunch I went back to my room. Jan called me and said he had ordered one of each tropical drink on the liquor menu, and we were invited to come to his room. I arrived about the same time as the table full of drinks—yet another beautiful sight. We toasted the islands, the surf, the tiki gods, the floral wallpaper, puka shells, the fine sailors that went down with the USS *Arizona*. Then Jan said he had some great news. Because of all the bad publicity we had

First photo of Jan Berry and Dean Torrence together,
University High School Warriors, 1956

First promotional photo of Jan & Dean
Hollywood, 1959

Second promotional photo of Jan & Dean
Hollywood, 1959

Dean, Lou Adler, Jan, and Herb Alpert
Hollywood Recording Studio, 1959

MUSIC VENDOR

AUG. 10
1959
No. 636

THE NATIONAL WEEKLY OF RECORDED MUSIC

25¢

Manager Lou Adler (without the milk) flanked by Jan (right) and Dean, DORE recording artists, whose "Baby Talk" (and such big boys, too!) is climbing on all the charts. (Story on page 24.)

STEREO
ON
SINGLES
See Page 3

The sign on the door read "no food in the studio please"

Promotional photo of Jan & Dean, 1964
Record executives were pissed because the treble clef was upside down

Top: Jan & Dean in concert, Seattle, Washington, 1965
Bottom: Hangin' at the Whiskey à GoGo, 1965

Echo Park, downtown Los Angeles, 1965
Jan is teaching them the vocal parts to "Sidewalk Surfin'"

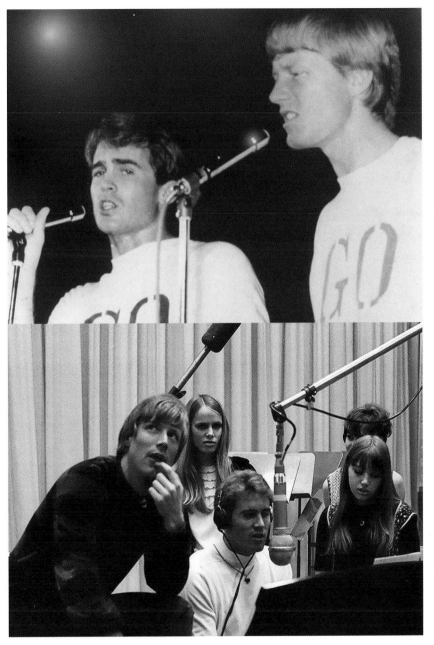

Top: Jan & Dean at the Whiskey à Go Go, 1965
Bottom: Jan & Dean in the Columbia Recording Studio, 1966

Jan in the Columbia Recording Studio, April 4, 1966
(*Photo by Dean*)

Jan in the Columbia Recording Studio, April 4, 1966
(*Photo by Dean*)

Jan's totaled Corvette Sting Ray, April 12, 1966

Stills of the filming of the TV movie, *Deadman's Curve*
(*Photos by Dean*)

Top: On stage with The Beach Boys, Three Rivers Stadium
Bottom: Our tour bus (*Photo by Carl Wilson*)

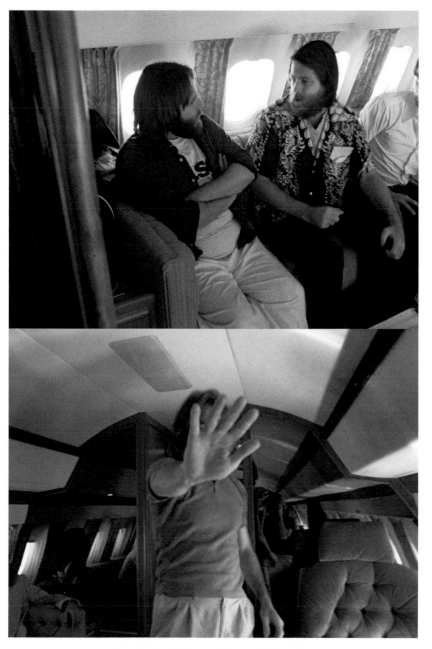

Top: Carl and Brian relaxing on the tour bus
Bottom: Dennis being Dennis (*Photos by Dean*)

Top: Promotional photo, 1981
Bottom: Jan at the Golden Bear, Huntington Beach (*Photo by Dean*)

just gotten because of the trial and being close friends with some kidnappers, we had been kicked off the movie, *Ride the Wild Surf.* We were screaming for joy. Yeah! We won't have to appear in that lame piece of shit movie. It was great news. We would have been the laughing stock of not only the surf community, but the rock community, too.

The only reason we had agreed to be in the film in the first place was to get the opportunity to write and record the movie title song "Ride the Wild Surf." Once we saw the first draft of the screenplay, we really wanted out of any of the filming. We had seen what had happened to Elvis's recording career as a direct result of not paying attention to the quality of projects being offered to him. Up to this point, we had resisted all the other lame beach movie offers, the very same ones that a few of our musician friends were appearing in.

We felt really sorry for Elvis. He was really a nice guy and a hell of a singer. Hal, by the way, had played on some of Elvis's recordings. Let's toast him! But for the life of us, we couldn't figure out why he allowed himself to be involved with such corny, mediocre film projects. That old fart, *The General.* Bet it was his idea. These films had the potential to totally ruin his credibility as a rock star, and for what purpose? He was already the King. What else was there? Let's toast the King!

"Hey, let's hope he doesn't do anything else stupid like play Las Vegas or something like that."

"Not Elvis! The King would never play Vegas, another toast!" We now got the brilliant idea to go for a drive. Yeah! Great idea. Let's go pick up our free Honda Scramblers (courtesy of our Beach Boys connection) and ride out to Makapu'u to do some body surfing until the sun sets. This was the life. What a difference a day makes, indeed!

Summer 1964 came and went. We had already had four major hits that year. "Dead Man's Curve" peaked the charts at number eight, "New Girl in School" at number thirty-seven, and "Little Old Lady from Pasadena" at number three. And "Ride the Wild Surf" had just peaked at number fifteen. Fall was now upon us. Each fall we would start our new football season by showing up at the University High School football field every Sunday afternoon to choose teams, and kick the crap out of one another. Most of us were high school football lettermen; some of us were currently on the Santa Monica City College football team, including me. Jan had considering trying out for the UCLA freshmen football team, which he could have easily made. In other words, we were all pretty damn good at football.

One Sunday Jan called to tell me that he had not been able to reach many of the guys and that we might not have enough players for two teams. I said I would make some calls to see who I could round up. The only guy I found at home was a high school kid my old girlfriend Cindy used to babysit, Bob Wood. Bob was not a great athlete by any stretch of the imagination, but he was big, really big, and in a pinch he was a big, wide body we could use to put on the line. At least we would have enough guys to play and that was the bottom line. I picked Bob up and drove him to the football field where we met up with all the other hopefuls. Damn—we had only enough for one and a half teams. We were very much in a mood to play ball so we waited in hopes that some of the others would straggle in, but it soon became apparent that no one else was going to show up.

We started thinking of alternatives. It was too late to show up at any of the other football fields. The only choice left, if we were bound and determined to play football that day, was to go to Beverly Glen Park. This was a real last resort. It was not really a football field, rather an oddly shaped park. Also, because there were always numerous teams waiting to play, the rules were that the first team to score two touchdowns was the winner, and the winner would stay on and the loser would walk. Now, under normal conditions, that would have been okay with us. We had a very good team. Once we got into a game, we would usually win and stay on as long as we wanted. But that was elsewhere, not at Beverly Glen Park, because all was not normal at Beverly Glen Park. Far from it.

One team, the TCB (Taking Care of Business) team, owned the park. They had some really good players to be sure, but as a team from top to bottom—except for Bob—we were better. But the TCB made up their own rules, and it was impossible for anyone other than them to win a game. We had tried before. Yes, we could beat them, but we could never win the game. That's why Beverly Glen Park was a last resort.

We jumped in our cars, drove up Bundy to Sunset, turned right, and drove by Dead Man's Curve, just above the UCLA practice fields. We could look down on the field and see that there were at least ten fraternity games being played as we drove by. We continued east on Sunset, past Bel Air until we came to Beverly Glen. We turned north and headed up the canyon and this canyon was beautiful, lots of great looking trees and beautiful homes. The park was only a few blocks off of Sunset. We parked. It looked crowded as usual, but we were committed.

We signed in and then found a place to stretch and throw the ball around. We noted that the home team was holding court as usual. I looked over just in time to see my old teammate from Santa Monica City College, who had just transferred to USC, Ron Heller, score a touchdown. Another team bites the dust—or grass. We continued to warm up.

Finally it was our turn to play. We met the home team at the middle of the field, said hi, shook hands, and flipped the coin. It was their coin, and they won, as usual, and they wanted the ball. We put our kickoff team on the field. They booted the ball down the field and the game was on. I was to play my usual defensive back spot, playing man-to-man coverage on the split end or playing zone coverage depending on TCB's game plan. Since I was the one who brought Bob, I had him play defensive end on my side of the field so I could help him get lined up. His job was to rush the passer on a pass play. Or on a running play to our side he was to force the runner to run inside of him and let our linebackers take care of the running back. And he had better not let anyone get outside of him or he would have to walk home.

The offense broke their huddle. They lined up. The quarterback looked over my way, so I moved up like I was going to play bump and run. He looked over to the other side, so I backed off. The ball was hiked. Ron Heller ran up the middle for a short game. Second down and long. A passing down most likely. I told Bob to rush the quarterback—don't even consider a running play. Head to the place the quarterback will drop back to throw the pass. He said okay. The ball was hiked. The split receiver who always got a lot of balls thrown his way ran a down and out on me. A running back brush-blocked Bob then snuck out into the flat in a delay pattern. I left my guy, came back, and with the help of our linebackers, we made the stop, but it was a first down. I could see Bob was unable to effectively rush the quarterback because he was too big and too slow.

So in our defensive huddle I told Bob to line up further out and to play just outside of Elvis's left outside shoulder, and when the ball is hiked, rush through his outside shoulder and push him into the backfield. That would give me some extra time to see if a second receiver was running a delay pattern to my side. I thought Bob's eyes were going to pop out. He was now looking over at the other team members who were just breaking their huddle and heading for the line of scrimmage. Bob was frozen.

Ah, Christ, I had just now realized Bob had no idea we had been playing Elvis Presley's TCB football team, and he had been lining up less than two feet away from the guy. It just hadn't occurred to me that this was important information. This, to me, was a football game, not a social event. I yelled at Bob that the play was about to start.

"Get up to the line and play where I asked you to play," I yelled. He was in a trance, staring at Elvis, who was now only a few feet away from him. The play started. Elvis ran a post pattern, but it was a run to the opposite side. Their running back ran down the sidelines. Our guys stopped, and he kept running. Touchdown! Our guys said, hey, he was out of bounds way back here. Elvis's bodyguard, Red West, came over to the spot where our guys said their guy was out of bounds. He looks down toward a tree some seventy-five yards down at the end of the park.

"Yah see that there tree down yonder? That one. Right there. Not that one, but that there one."

"Which tree you talking about, Red, they all kinda look alike."

"Well that one right there with the one big limb. Line up that tree with the trash can right there in back of us, and you can clearly see this spot is still in bounds. Well, yes, it is close I know, but we were in bounds." The touchdown stands.

"Ready to receive the kickoff gentlemen?" I looked for Bob. He is still pretty much where he was when the play began, still staring at Elvis. We received the kickoff and our best runner, Sonny Minachello, almost took it all the way back for a touchdown. But Red West says Sonny had run out of bounds way back yonder upfield. Say what?

"You said line up that tree with that trash can. He was clearly in bounds." Red looked down at the tree.

"Nah, you got it wrong. Now on this sideline we don't use the tree, you line up the trashcan with the pole that the street sign is on. That's the sideline on this side of the field."

We huddle up, pissed off. We all agree that we can't win the game, so let's just kick some ass. Let's do a student body right on three. I love sweeps. We have great blockers who loved creaming people, and Sonny was a real quick shifty runner. My assignment on a sweep to my side was to split out, and when the play starts do a crackback block on the first person I come to, usually an outside linebacker that is assigned to stop the run.

The defensive back covering me thinks I am running a slant pattern, and he follows me, so I occupy two guys. This leaves the whole sidelines open for Sonny with only maybe a safety to contend with—and anyone one-on-one with Sonny will lose. The play starts. I look to my inside and there is a Hollywood-looking guy in a lavender turtleneck sweater. Yum, yum. Elvis's team did win the best-dressed award every weekend. He is standing flat-footed, waiting for Sonny to commit. When Sonny finally commits to the outside, I arrive. He never saw me coming. I hit him shoulder high and he went down in a heap in the mud. Sonny flew by us, untouched, into the end zone. We all looked at Red waiting for him to find some reason why it wasn't a touchdown. He went off the field. Maybe he had to check with Elvis—Elvis didn't play defense. Maybe Elvis saw something Red missed. Red stayed on the sidelines so we assumed we were awarded the touchdown.

We lined up to kickoff. The score was now seven to seven. We kicked the ball and stopped them pretty deep in their own territory. I brought Bob back into the game, asked him if he was ready to play and not stargaze. He said he was, but he just couldn't and wouldn't block Elvis—anybody else, but not Elvis. So I had Bob flip-flop with the other defensive end who was drooling for the opportunity to pop the King. Dave Dillon was at least 6′ 3″, 220 pounds and very quick and physical, but a clean player—no cheap shots.

Dave lined up just off Elvis's outside shoulder. The ball snapped. Dave knocked Elvis on his butt, and then pursued the quarterback. The quarterback quickly dumped the ball off to his safety valve receiver for a short gain. Elvis was a class act. He brushed himself off and rejoined the huddle. None of Elvis's teammates gave Dave any dirty looks. They knew it was a clean play and they left it at that. The next play Elvis took a much wider split. If Dave split out that far he would not be able to get the quarterback as quickly as before, so Dave moved back inside to rush the quarterback, and I was once again one-on-one with Elvis. He ran a quick slant over the middle. The quarterback threw the ball perfectly. Elvis caught it, and was tattooed by our very physical middle linebacker, Ivory Jones, a former UCLA linebacker.

Even though Elvis hit the ground hard, he held on to the ball. Once again he got up, brushed the grass and mud off, and headed back to the huddle. His teammates also treated it as just another football play. How very cool, but I had bit on a head fake move Elvis had made to the outside. I bit on that move to an "out" pattern because I was convinced he didn't have the nerve to run a pass pattern to the inside over the middle where many hardnosed guys were waiting to get a piece of the King. He fooled me. Well done, Mr. Presley.

TCB, of course, went on to win the game—although there was some controversy about their game-winning second touchdown. Their guy had run into the street and come back into the end zone. Red was right there to explain that in this particular end zone, since the park was a trapezoid, it was ok to go out in the street and then come back. It was the other end zone, that one over yonder in back of us, where you weren't allowed to use the street. Guess we confused one end for the other. Sorry, gentlemen. Thanks for the game. We all shook hands. I shook hands with Elvis and said, "Good game." He said the same and that is the last time I ever saw him in person again.

As I said, all was not normal at Beverly Glen Park—in fact, it was far from it.

5

SoCAL CAR CULTURE

{1964}

Jan and I loved cars so we thought it might be time to move on from surf songs, at least for the moment. This would give us a lot more range in terms of subject matter related to Southern California car culture. So using the "Surf City" template, which seemed to work okay, we started working on a song called "Drag City." Jan once again got Brian Wilson involved, and he also asked a disc jockey friend, Roger Christian, to help write the song. In the studio, Jan sang the lead, and Brian and I sang the "Whine, whine, whine" parts that I wrote. Then Brian and I sang the very cool falsetto part that Brian wrote. Jan put the finishing touches on the background vocals with his also very cool bass part. We added on some sound effects from the San Fernando Drag Strip and we had finished our first car song.

The single "Drag City" was released November 8, 1963. On the flip side was a song that ended up being one of my all-time favorites, "Schlock Rod." The song was just a filler on the *Drag City* album so we didn't pay much attention to it in the studio. The weakest songs on an album always got recorded last because you would save your energy for the better songs that had obvious potential.

So Jan and I were in the studio hoping to finish the vocals on the last song to get recorded for the *Drag City* album. This song, "Schlock Rod," was originally titled "Bean Wagon," which was the name used for a Mexican lowrider. We were pretty sure our record company would freak out if we recorded a song titled "Bean Wagon" so we changed the title to "Schlock Rod." It was late at night and we had already been in the studio most of the day finishing other songs. Now we were faced with this one last song, the one we had been putting off. We were burnt out and ready to go home.

We tried to sing it, but the song really sucked. Finally I suggested that we just talk instead of singing the damn thing, kind of like "Alley-Oop," which had been a number one song back in 1960. Talking it would take a lot less time and we could improvise all we wanted to. Hey, we could even throw in some sound effects for good measure. Jan pointed out that finding sound effects at this hour of the night would take way too long, so we should just find crap in the studio that we could use. Bones, our engineer, started the tape, and we immediately kicked over a bunch of metal chairs that crashed to the ground. Then we alternated talking the verses and improvised most of the song. We cracked each other up, which made it so much fun that we let the song just keep going. The song was so long that it ended up being part one and part two. On the album "Schlock Rod Part One" ends side one and "Schlock Rod Part Two" is the first song on side two. I am not sure that this had ever been done before.

The single "Drag City" ended up being our third top-ten record in a row. The *Drag City* album, which was one of my favorite albums, ended up being our first top-twenty album.

Our next single "Dead Man's Curve" was also on the Drag City album, but we had rushed to finish the song and Jan really wanted to spend some more time on the recording to make it even better. And that he did. "Dead Man's Curve" was his masterpiece. The production was brilliant, his arrangement was brilliant, and the execution of the layers of vocals was second to none. It had horns, it had strings, it had castanets—it even had a harp. I think it's safe to say, these instruments were not featured on your typical rock-and-roll record in the sixties. "Dead Man's Curve" was our fourth top 10 record in a row.

On our "Dead Man's Curve" album we recorded a very silly song that I co-wrote titled "Bucket T." It was a distant cousin to Jan & Arnie's "Jenny Lee." Unbeknownst to us, some equally silly sods from "across the pond" who were big Jan & Dean fans were so inspired by "Bucket T" that they recorded their own version of the song. I bet you are asking who and you're right—The Who featured it on their hit album *Magic Bus* and the biggest Jan & Dean fan of all, Keith Moon, sang lead on their recording.

Well the car songs seem to be working for us so why not create another one. Our old buddy from high school, Don Altfeld, who had collaborated on writing many Jan & Dean songs, had seen a local Southern California Dodge dealer's commercial featuring a little old lady driving a Super Stock Dodge. He and Jan were in medical school together, so Don finds Jan at school the next day to tell him about this very clever, very amusing TV commercial. They decide there and then to write a song about this hot rodding grandma. Jan admitted that he and Don would sit in lectures together and work on the lyrics to the song. It now had a title, "The Little Old Lady from Pasadena." What a cool song. It had a great hook, a really good melody, and it had the Jan & Dean humor front and center.

Jan cut an awesome track with some really solid horn parts. He had put his reference lead vocal on the track with one of our background singers, Phil Sloan, doing some of the background parts. I came to the studio the next night to finish the background harmony parts. While I was recording I always wanted to hear the lead vocal plus the track in my earphones. The song had three verses, and they were pretty much alike. So I was singing one of the harmony parts and I get to the third verse, and Jan's vocal drops out but reappears in the last half of the third verse. It didn't throw me off so I kept singing till the end. Jan said he liked it and for me to come into the control room to listen and make sure it was okay. After we listened to it and decided to keep it, I told Jan about his lead vocal dropping out half way through the third verse, then reappearing on the line "The guys come to race her from all around, but she gives them a length and she shuts them down." My suggestion was to leave the lead vocal out just like I heard it and then bring it back in just like I heard it.

"What about the melody?" he asked.

I said, "Why not have an instrument play the melody? That way all three verses are not alike."

"What kind of instrument?"

"A harmonica," I said. Jan said I needed to add one more vocal to the block harmonies, so I went back into the studio to do my vocal. Maybe twenty minutes later Jan said it sounded great. I went into the control room to listen. While we were listening to the playback the phone rang and Bones, our engineer, answered. He hung up the phone and said to Jan, "He's on his way." I asked who was coming here at 1:30 a.m., and Jan said the harmonica player.

A little side note: We had given our pals The Beach Boys a demo of "The Little Old Lady from Pasadena" a few weeks earlier because they wanted to include our next single on their upcoming live album. We forgot to give them a heads-up about changing the song, so they recorded our old version. If you are interested in hearing the original version, dig out The Beach Boys Live album recorded in Sacramento. It's a totally different song without the harmonica. "Little Old Lady from Pasadena" ended up being our fifth top 10 record in a row.

About a year later, I was fortunate enough to be in the right place at the right time. Jan and I were in a studio at Western Recorders and The Beach Boys were in a studio next door working on their *Party* album. We were invited to participate on that record, but our record company wanted a signed contract from The Beach Boys saying that they would officially participate on a future Jan & Dean album. We said that we had an oral agreement, and that's all we needed. The suits said that it wasn't good enough and if we participated, they would hold up our royalties. Jan had just bought a new house so he capitulated. I, on the other hand, still lived at home with my parents so I didn't give a shit what the suits said.

Jan and I were working on some ballad at the time that I really didn't care for. Later I was quoted saying that the song was "You Really Know How to Hurt a Guy," which was another song I didn't care for so I probably used "Hurt a Guy" as a metaphor for that kind of sappy ballad. Don't get me wrong, Jan's production of these songs was as good as it gets, but I just didn't think it fit the Jan & Dean brand to be singing this kind of sappy ballad. Nevertheless, I was there in the studio to put my vocal on it, if that's what Jan wanted. So while Jan was finishing up a vocal part he was working on, I said I was going next door to say hello to the boys and I would be right back. He said okay but I had better not sing on it. I said he shouldn't worry, I didn't want to get sued either.

When I walked into the studio the guys said, "Hey, want to sing something?" I said sure I do. They rattled off some songs they were thinking of doing, but I knew most of them would take some rehearsing and I didn't have that much time. I tried to think of an easy song to do that would have some fun doo-wops.

"Hey what about 'Barbara Ann'?" I said. "Jan & Dean did a version of it four year earlier and almost put it out as a single—let's do Barbara Ann." We did three takes. The first two takes I sang the falsetto in the block harmonies with Mike, Carl, Dennis, and

Bruce. The third take Brian wanted me to sing with him. There was a little tug-of-war between the background singers and Brian, but Brian was the big kahuna so he won and I sang with him. Meanwhile I am looking at my watch. Okay, let's do it. Take three is a winner. I wasn't worried because all our voices sounded alike, so who was to know. I thanked the guys and headed back to Jan. I had been gone for maybe ten to twelve minutes.

Think about that, in ten to twelve minutes we recorded the second best-selling single The Beach Boys ever recorded.

6
GOING BIG TIME

{1964–1966}

Jan was now our record producer and we were still full-time college students. I had transferred to USC. I was in The School of Architecture and Fine Arts studying Advertising Design and Jan had graduated from UCLA and he was now in med school at The California College of Medicine in downtown Los Angeles. This didn't leave much for Lou to do with Jan & Dean in terms of record producing or personal management duties anymore. So Lou, realizing that we had a lot more potential in other areas that he only had limited expertise in, began looking for a non-musical management company for us. A company that, in turn, was maybe looking to branch off into more music related projects. And Lou found just the guys—Bobby Roberts and Pierre Cossette. They were in the movie and television business. Lou offered to deliver Jan & Dean to Cossette and Roberts, who would actively try to develop movie and television projects for us. In turn, Lou would help build them a record company that he could head—with their money, of course.

Bobby Roberts had broken into show business as a dancer. He used the word "hoofer." He danced in a dance troupe called the Dunhills, so they decided to call their record company Dunhill

Records. They brought an old experienced record company guy, Jay Lasker, on board to be the president and in charge of administration. Lou would be the creative guy and look for new talent to bring to the label. Over on the other side of town, Herb Alpert and his new partner, Jerry Moss, were continuing to build a very successful and profitable multimillion-dollar record company known as A&M Records. I'm sure Lou was hoping to build a company that would give A&M a run for its money and show his old friend Herbie that he, too, was capable of achieving the same kind of success. Also part of Lou's duties was to develop a music publishing company to work hand in hand with Dunhill Records. Lou had come upon two young singer/songwriters, Steve Berri and Phil Sloan. These two kids thought it was cool that Lou worked with Jan & Dean and really wanted to write some surf songs for Jan & Dean.

So Lou gave them the green light to see what they could come up with. Within a couple of days they returned to the office with "Tell 'em I'm Surfin'" and "Summer Means Fun." Meanwhile, Cossette and Roberts were looking to get us some nontraditional (for rock musicians) television exposure. These guys were well-connected. One of the first TV shows they booked us on was the very first *Dean Martin Show*. Being the debut show, Dean Martin had the whole rat pack on: Frank Sinatra, Peter Lawford, Sammy Davis Jr., and Joey Bishop. Jan and I were the only outsiders. With such a strong lineup, Dean Martin didn't really need us on his show, but there we were, all the same. It was also apparent that Frank Sinatra held no grudges towards me—though I wouldn't have blamed him if he had. I was really happy that we were accepted into their family, at least for that night. Mr. Sinatra could have very easily told Dean Martin to give us the boot, but he chose not to.

Before the taping of the show, we were invited to Dean Martin's dressing room to meet everyone. They were all really nice guys and loads of fun. Mr. Sinatra was cordial. He shook my hand but didn't have anything to say to me, which was okay with me. I was just happy to shake his hand. He was very friendly to Jan, whom he had met many times before. Jan and Nancy Sinatra were classmates, and Jan had visited Nancy at the Sinatra's Bel Air home.

Peter Lawford, on the other hand, shook my hand, looked inquisitively at me and said, "Have we met before? You look very familiar to me."

I said, "Does 21457 Beverly Glen, Apt. C, refresh your memory?" His face turned red.

"Oh, that was you? Oh, God." I told him that it was our secret. He said thank you and he went off looking for his wife.

Jan said, "What was that all about?"

"Well, you remember Sonnie's apartment? She lived at 21457 Beverly Glen in an apartment complex that had a courtyard. Her apartment, Apt. A, faced the courtyard and an apartment door on the other side of the courtyard, Apt. C. I used to sneak out of her apartment in the middle of the night, usually carrying my shoes. I would say that six, seven, maybe eight times I would come face-to-face with this other guy also trying to steal away into the night carrying his shoes. We would nod at one another, kind of smile, get in our cars, and drive off. I'm sure he was hoping that in the darkness I wasn't able to recognize him, but I did. It was Peter Lawford. Oh, naughty, naughty boy. Now I was sneaking out to go home to my own bed at my parent's house. My shoes were off so as not to disturb my parents. I doubt he was doing the same." Jan laughed.

One of the next TV shows our new managers got us was *The Red Skeleton* Easter show. Big time stuff. We showed up at a rehearsal where they informed us that we were to sing the Easter Parade song—straight. We were really concerned about this. We had just been proclaimed by some rock media person to be the "clown princes of rock and roll." Now I ask you, would the newly crowned "clown princes of rock and roll" sing the Easter Parade song—straight? I think not.

They sent us to wardrobe where we were to be fitted with tuxedos with tails. Then they wanted us to wear patent leather shoes with spats. I said no way, I don't wear leather shoes. I only wear sneakers. Period. They conferred. Oh, what if we put the spats over the sneakers? That was bizarre looking. Yeah, I like it. They then took us to the set for a dress rehearsal and a run-through of the song. They gave us top hats. We said we ain't wearing these. They'll fuck up our hair. They said okay, you don't have to wear the hats, you can hold them. Then they gave us canes and started the music. We were to lip sync and work out some simple choreography. Jan looked great in a tux. I didn't. So I instinctively let him take the lead and I tried to make it appear as though I were trying to mirror what he was doing, always being about a beat behind him. It was a funny bit. Well, I thought it was funny.

The music stopped and the director comes over and says, "Um, you look uncomfortable doing this number."

I said, "Yes, I know I look uncomfortable. That's the whole friggin' idea you moron." I kinda of mumbled the last part.

"Let's try it again, gentlemen." Well, I wasn't about to do it straighter. If anything, I took the bit even further. The music stopped again. The director came to me and said, "You still look very confused about what to do with your hat and cane."

"That's the whole idea," I said, and then mumbled "asshole." He walked off into the dark set. We stood there and stood there and stood there waiting for the music to come back on.

Then out of the darkness appears Bobby Roberts, obviously out of breath, sweating, and looking somewhat panicked.

"What are you doing here, Bobby?"

"The director called me at my office and said we have a problem. You better get over here right now. So what's going on?"

I told him that if we are the "clown princes of rock and roll" we sure as hell can't be asked to do this Easter parade thing straight. No way. We won't do it. We will be fucking up our branding, and on top of that, what would Keith Moon say? Bobby leaves to go talk to the director. A few minutes later he comes back and says, "Okay you can goof it some but just don't overdo it. And please remember that Red Skeleton is the comedian here. And this is his show. You shouldn't try to upstage him. You will have your chance another day, I promise you. Okay?"

"Okay."

A few weeks later Bobby calls us to the office to tell us about another new project. It was a brilliant concept—a musical concert with many different acts on the same stage to be filmed on something like videotape called Electrovision. The final product would then be shown theatrically in movie theaters all over the world. It was to be called the *T.A.M.I. Show (Teenage Awards Music International).* And get this, Jan & Dean would not only be performing with groups like The Rolling Stones, The Beach Boys, The Supremes, Marvin Gay, Chuck Berry, James Brown, and the Flames—they would also be the hosts, write and perform the title songs, and do stunts in the opening titles. It sounded like a great project. We were stoked.

One of the first elements we worked on was the opening titles. It was to be a montage of action shots, a lot of us mixed with shots of the other groups. The title song was being written by our new friends Steve Barri and Phil Sloan and it was titled, "(Here They Come) from All Over the World." The opening verse of the song was, "They're coming from all over the world." So the idea was to film all the artists arriving on all sorts of different types of transportation. Jan and I got to pick out what we wanted to do. We skateboarded across a busy Sunset Boulevard right next to the Whisky a Go Go and then crashed right in front of the Santa Monica Civic Auditorium, which was going to be the concert venue. We also rode motorcycles on Sunset through Beverly Hills. But the real thrill for me was when we got to drive a couple of dual engine, state-of-the-art go-carts. We raced around the parking lot of the Santa Monica Civic Auditorium until the cops came and shut us down. But I was already hooked.

A couple of days later I was talking to Dennis Wilson at one of the rehearsals for the *T.A.M.I. Show*. Dennis and I had a mutual passion for fast cars. We had on many occasions met at San Fernando Drag Strip for grudge races. I had a midnight blue 427 Stingray with big drag racing slicks on the back. Dennis had just bought a Shelby 427 Cobra. It was a very quick car. I don't remember much about the official on-track grudge matches, but as far as I recall, we were pretty evenly matched. I do, however, remember the drives home after the official races. That is when the real racing started.

It was a street race all the way through the San Fernando Valley, at every stoplight, until we got to Sepulveda Pass. Then it was a race up the valley side through the tunnel, just like at Monaco. Then we would fly down the other side of the mountain towards Sunset Boulevard, where we would turn off, go balls-out heading east past the Bel Air gate, through Dead Man's Curve just above UCLA, then down towards Beverly Glen where I would peel off, wave good-bye, and head home. There was one time when an older guy in a black Corvette made it a three-way race on Sunset. Shit, he was very, very quick. We all came to a stop at a red light together. Dennis and I looked over to see who was pushing us so hard. Oh, shit! That's James Garner, star of the Formula One movie, *Grand Prix*! I chickened out and turned right. I called Dennis later to see if he was still living. He said he had smoked Garner. I believed him.

Anyway, we were hanging around in our dressing rooms at the *T.A.M.I. Show* rehearsal and I very excitedly told him about my exhilarating afternoon racing around in the huge Santa Monica Civic parking lot in a dual engine go-cart and that I was thinking of getting one. He said, "Oh, I already have one of those. It needs some work. I wrecked it, but if you want to fix it you can borrow it."

"Man you are on. I'll pick it up tomorrow," I said. And I did.

This led me to not only fixing Dennis's go-cart, but buying two of my very own. Then he had to have two, because one always broke down. Now we had a problem—transporting four go-carts, plus parts, extra wheels, and the electronic starter. So I bought a white Chevy van and had custom racks made inside to hold the carts and equipment. We were so cool.

So what dramatic impact did the *T.A.M.I. Show* have on me? Was it meeting the Rolling Stones? Having a beer with James Brown? Seeing Diana Ross half-dressed? Trying not to see Leslie Gore half-dressed? Trying to shake the hand of the one-handed drummer in the group, The Barbarians? Getting paid all those big bucks? Hell, no. I got to go on my first go-cart ride!

Bobby Roberts had more big plans for us—a movie project. Not a guest shot like a lot of our friends were doing. This would be our own movie that we would star in and other established comedian actors would costar in. Wow! How cool! Basically it was a comedy with some special effects, and just a little bit of music. That suited us just fine.

We were to meet at the producer's house in Beverly Hills to read through the first draft of the screenplay. While waiting for some of the costars to show up, we did a quick read through. We were a little disappointed—it was okay, but not great. But then the real comedians showed up: Mel Brooks, Stan Freeberg, Terry Thomas, Don Knotts, and Jerry Lester and they made it come alive. It really was funny when real pros read the lines. We were all in tears. What a loony bunch of characters. This project was going to be a lot of fun to do with these guys.

In the script there was a scene where the origin of Jan & Dean was to be explained. That's right folks. Jan & Dean actually started out as two blind, black, soft-shoe dancing orphans and, being blind, we didn't know we were white. This is a little known fact. It was therefore arranged that we should be given some dance lessons so we could be just good enough to look like we had at least some knowledge of how to soft-shoe dance in the movie. There was a scene in the movie where we were to be booed off the stage at the Apollo by a very hostile group of black people and that's when we decided to become white singing surfers instead— obviously a career in a major transition. (I have a vague recollection that a few years later, I may have told my friend Steve Martin about this scene).

We were on summer vacation, so every day we would show up at the Paramount Studio lot where we would meet our dance teacher and do two hours of dancing. Hey, I thought, what would Keith Moon say about that? One day, a cute, long-legged blond teenage girl recognized us in the parking lot. She introduced herself as Edie—Edie Baskin. She asked us what we were doing there. We told her about our dancing lessons in Bungalow C. "Come by and visit us sometime," I said. The next day she dropped by Bungalow C with about twenty-five tourists, mostly Asians with cameras. Edie had forgotten to tell us she was a studio tour guide. She got great pleasure out of embarrassing us in front of all of these starstruck tourists.

Eventually we learned her shift timing and we would start looking out the window at a certain time to see her arriving at the bungalow with her herd of wide-eyed tourists. We would tell our dance teacher we had to take a piss and then bolt out the back door until she had finally moved on. It was a great game.

7

THE GREAT TRAIN WRECK

{1965}

I t was finally time to start filming. We were given a final draft of the *Easy Come, Easy Go* script. Lou and Bobby had these beautiful leather binders made up to hold our scripts with our names in gold leaf on the front. They also put notes inside saying how proud of us they were, and good luck. Break a leg. Break a leg? I wonder what that meant.

We met up with our limo and driver at the employee parking lot at Paramount Studios and then drove out to the desert community of Chatsworth. This was where we were going to film the final scene of the movie. It was all visual stuff—no lines were involved, so this was going to be fun. The scene called for us to walk on some railroad tracks where we would end up being run over by a locomotive. Then the special effects guys and animators would make little pieces out of us and a gust of wind would blow our pieces down the track. Totally bitchin' stuff as far as we were concerned, kinda like a music video except we had never seen a music video. They didn't exist yet. We thought this was much better than singing a duet with Ann-Margret or Shelley Fabares, or duking it out with some Hollywood version of the Hells Angels on a beach covered with surfboards and pasty-skinned, overly hair-sprayed Hollywood starlets in bathing suits.

We arrived to a bustling location, lots of trucks and people. Man this was for real. The director, Barry Shear, met us as soon as we stepped out of the limo. "Good morning gentlemen, let's go to work." He sat down with us to go through what the first shot was about. This scene was to be from the locomotive's point of view initially. The locomotive would see us walking way up the tracks with our backs to it. The fast moving locomotive would get closer and closer. At some point we would hear it quickly approaching. We would turn, looking back over our shoulders, and then take off running on the tracks. It would continue to close in on us rapidly. We were to continue to run as fast as we could until it got too close; then we were to peel off and let the train pass by. Of course they would edit out us leaving the tracks. Sounds cool. Let's shoot it CB (short for Cecil B. DeMille).

We were sent to the makeup trailer, and a very effeminate man put some makeup on us and off we went to be in our first movie. We strolled out onto the railroad tracks where there was a flatcar with a camera mounted on the front of it. There was also a team of crewmembers on the flatcar—the cameraman, the director, the assistant director, the script lady, some studio grips and more railroad personnel, plus some union dudes. The flatcar was coupled to a very serious Santa Fe locomotive. The director said "Slate it. Let's do it." The locomotive started, backing down the track towing the flatcar. They were to back up at least half a mile and then would stop, turn on the big light on the locomotive, and that would mean they were rolling in our direction. The locomotive was now pushing the flatcar with the camera towards us. We were to start walking with our backs toward the locomotive and the camera. Hot damn! We are now officially in show business!

The locomotive lights were on—time to walk. Since there was no sound, we could talk about anything we wanted. "Who will get Edie's phone number first?" was the question of the day. The real question of the day should have been obvious, "How close is that train to us?" But we wanted to be macho guys and not look back too soon.

"How old do you think she is? You think she has a boyfriend?" We could now hear the train.

"That's a good question. We should ask her, if we ever see her again." The train sounds really close, but I didn't want to be the first to turn around and look.

Jan looked, and said, "It's time to run!" We ran for some fifty yards or so and the train was getting very close, and it was going fast. We finally peeled off and the train went whizzing by. It stopped and backed all the way up to the original starting place. The director said it looked great, but just to be sure and be on the safe side, let's shoot it one more time. Okay by us. We had sweat a little, so he told us to go back to makeup while they backed up to their staging point.

We sat down in the makeup chair. The makeup guy was livid. He called the director a jerk-off and a litany of other names. We asked what had the director had done to piss him off.

"What did he do? You haven't a clue, do you?" No we didn't. He went on to say that what we had just done would have been considered dangerous even by professional stuntmen standards.

"That little television director jerk-off is way out of his league. You guys could have easily been injured or even killed. You need to tell him you will not do it again, damn it!" He finished the makeup and we headed back to the tracks.

Hey, if they had told us they wanted to use stuntmen, we would have told them to go film a Frankie Avalon movie. Jan & Dean always do their own stunts!

On goes the light. Take two is underway. This time we let the train get even closer. The director loved it and was ready to shoot the next scene. We were not involved in the next scene since they needed to film what it all looked like from our point of view—the front of the locomotive getting closer and closer until the frame is filled with the front of the locomotive and its lights blazing. So they said in the next scene the flatcar will be pulled by the locomotive, and a second locomotive will approach them and get as close to the camera on the flatcar as possible. The flatcar would then try to duplicate our speed from walking to running. We were invited to be with the crew on the flatcar. Sure, why not? We got the dangerous part done. This scene is easy.

The flatcar starts to move at walking speed. The chase locomotive's light goes on. He's rolling. The assistant director has a two-way radio through which he is in contact with the approaching locomotive. They say he and the director will make the decisions about when to start accelerating and how much to accelerate. Then they will tell a Santa Fe employee standing in back of them what they want. He will use hand signals to communicate with the engineer of our train. You see, they said, the second set of two-way radios didn't work. So the old hand signal thing would have to do. Don't worry, they do it all the time. They are professionals.

By now, the approaching locomotive was closing in on us. The director asked for a little more speed. The approaching locomotive was still bearing down on us. The director asked for a little more speed. He got too much. We started to pull away. The director yelled, "Cut! Let's try it again." Both trains came to a stop and then backed up to their original starting points. The director told everyone we needed to get as close to each other as possible. The light goes on. The other train is rolling towards us again. This time one of the acceleration hand signals is interpreted to slow down. Holy shit! This didn't seem to be a great idea. Slow down when the guy chasing you is still accelerating and you are both on the same track? Frantically, the signal is sent to quickly accelerate. We start to pull away again. "Cut! Cut! Cut! Let's do it again people, and let's get it right. We need to get really close."

Now we are backing up again. I think I have an idea. And shit, man, I am one of the stars. I approach the director. "Say, don't you guys have a zoom lens? Just zoom the front of the locomotive up when you see it is not getting any closer."

"Dean, please go sit down. I am the director and I don't have time to explain each and every one of my decisions to you. Okay?" I take my seat. A few minutes later he comes over to me. "Sorry, Dean, I didn't mean to snap at you. Yes, we have a zoom lens, but the problem with zooming is that the background zooms up as well. That's why zooming, in this case, would not work. Okay?" I accepted his apology, but I really wanted to tell him how a zoom lens worked and I was certainly aware that whatever was in the background would also come forward. But I am looking at the background and it's a beautiful, typical California day out in the desert. Clear blue skies. No clouds. No trees. Not even a cactus and no mountains. What was there in the background to be pulled up in the zoom? Oh well, time for me to think about something more important—lunch.

We were pulling up to the location camp. I decided to get off the flatcar. I asked Jan if he wanted to walk back up the tracks because I saw a service road where I thought I saw an A&W Rootbeer stand. Jan looked at his watch and said the catered lunch was being served in less than an hour, and why not wait for that since it's free. I said I didn't feel like waiting, so I'd see him later, and off I went. I was the only one to get off of the flatcar. I started walking along the side of the tracks toward the oncoming locomotive. A few minutes up the track, the chase locomotive whizzes by me. I remember thinking, man that sucker is big and it's going very fast . . . Man I can't wait to have a frosty root beer float.

Kaboom! I was afraid to look when I heard the crash. I turned around to see how bad it was. Oh, shit. It looked bad! The dust and smoke were still rising, and people from the location site were all running towards the crash site. People that had been in cars that had been held up at the crossing were out of their cars, and they too were running toward the crash site. I was a good mile or more up the tracks. I started running back towards the wreck. For some reason I was laughing as I was running. I think I was just so very happy I was not lying crumpled up on that hot desert sand. But as I got closer I started to feel sick to my stomach. A car driving on the sand passed me going the other way. As I looked over at it, Jan leaned out the window and shouted at me, "I broke my leg. I'm going to the hospital."

Now I was really sick to my stomach. I continued running. I could now see what had happened. The chase locomotive had indeed run into the flatcar. The impact had lifted one end of the flatcar way off the ground, and the locomotive was kind of burrowed underneath it. The flatcar had stayed relatively horizontal and level, but it had been pushed to a pretty radical vertical angle. It was pretty obvious that if the flatcar had gone up and then turned over off the track, people would have been crushed and killed by it.

The first person I came up on was, yes, you guessed it, the director. He was face down in the sand. It looked like his shoulder and collarbone were broken. He was having trouble breathing. I asked him what he would like me to do. He wanted his face and nose out of the sand, so I picked his head up just enough to slip a towel under his head and then turned his head so he was no longer face down in the sand. I asked if he wanted me to move his shoulder. He said no. He did say he was very hot, so I looked around for something to cover him from the direct sunlight. I spotted a script laying a few feet away. I had the feeling it was no longer going to be needed. I started ripping out the pages and placing them on top of him. As it turned out, the title page ended up on his head—okay I admit it, I had something to do with its placement. It just seemed fitting to see this page there because the title had been written in big bold letters, EASY COME, EASY GO.

The ambulance came and took away seventeen people. I invited everybody left at the crash site back to the location site where the catering guys had already set up lunch. We had seventeen extra lunch settings. Hey, nothing like a good train wreck to perk up the old appetite, I've always said. We had cops, people from the cars, press, photographers, railroad people, old prospectors, and hippies from the Spawn Ranch. Sometime during the lunch I look around and my eyes met the eyes of our makeup buddy. "I told you so," he said.

I found the limo driver and the two of us drove back to Hollywood. He dropped me off back at the VIP parking lot at Paramount Studios. As I was getting into my car, Edie comes running over. She was very upset about what she had heard on the radio. I assured her that no one had died. Everybody would recover and maybe we would finish the film next summer. She said she couldn't wait until next summer to see us again, so she gave me her phone number. "Let's get together sometime," she said. I said, "Sure Edie. I'd like that." She went back to work, and I decided to hit the beach and play some volleyball while the sun was still up. As I put Edie's phone number in my glove compartment, I smiled, thinking of the conversation on the railroad track that Jan and I had only just a few hours ago. Man, how quickly things change.

8
JAN & DEAN VS. THE MONKEES

{1965}

While Jan was recovering from the compound fracture of his right leg, our management company was finalizing the details for a TV pilot project we were to star in. If this pilot was picked up, we would be staring in our very own TV series, and there were no trains involved.

At the same time, our associate record production company, Screen Gems, was developing their own television show titled *The Monkees*. We would both debut the same upcoming season on different networks. We were on ABC and The Monkees were going to be on NBC. We probably would not have gone head-to-head on the same night, at the same time slot, but there would have been some heavy promotional competition for market shares. It was expected we would have a big advantage over them by the obvious fact we were already an established, legitimate, successful rock group with an impressive string of major hit records spanning almost seven years. Plus we had a very large fan base and a very active fan club. Our good buddies, The Beach Boys, also said they would love to do some special guest appearances on our show. The Monkees were unknowns with no musical history whatsoever.

We understood that Screen Gems had the power and the material and eventually The Monkees would have hits. We could count on it. But we would have a big head start and we were determined to keep our advantage. Because of the severity of the compound fracture of Jan's leg, he had to take a leave of absence from medical school. We were also stressing out about getting his leg healed enough to get his big bulky cast off his leg in time to shoot the pilot. A rock star hobbling around on crutches would look bogus. We discussed delaying the shooting of the pilot, but then we took the chance of not getting the show on the next season's lineup, thereby giving the Monkees a season head start. It was decided not to take that chance, even if it meant that we would still have Jan in a cast. We would just have to go for it. And that is what we eventually did.

They tried to shoot around the cast, or should I say, above the cast. It was a hassle, but we had no other good options. A lot of this pilot was shot on location with real live high-intensity concert footage, shot with handheld cameras. This was something The Monkees could not duplicate, at least for now. We had never shot a TV pilot before. It was a lot of work and took up a lot of time. We would start shooting early in the morning and not finish until late at night. We were exhausted.

After the last night of shooting, we went back to our hotel to relax. The rest of the cast and crew were all getting together in the bar for a "wrap party" but we were too tired. I remember sitting in Jan's room feeling really happy about the fact that we were done shooting, but distressed over the probability of having to do a bunch more of these. I had a sense Jan might be experiencing the same kind of thoughts. I finally got around to asking Jan if he knew how much money we would be making if this pilot got picked up for a season. It did seem like a strange time to be getting around to asking that question, this being the last night of shooting and all.

Jan was pretty sure we would be making what the top paying TV guys, the Smothers Brothers, were getting—$20,000 a show. I wanted to know if that was for each guy or what? Jan was pretty sure it was $20,000 for both of them, $10,000 each. I asked him if he thought Dick got more than Tommy because he was smarter, and his mom liked him better. Jan said, "What?"

"Why are we doing this anyway?" I asked. I pointed out that we had just worked off and on for almost two weeks from 7 a.m. until 8 p.m. for $10,000. Now compare that to the fact that we play concerts on weekends for $10,000 per night, or $20,000 per weekend. And all we have to do is show up for a sound check in the late afternoon, look for a good place to eat in the early evening, get dressed, have a few tropical drinks, and play a concert for about an hour and then concentrate on finding some girls to flirt with. And we wanted to trade that for this TV shit? I didn't get it.

Jan thought about it a few minutes. "Do you think it would be in bad taste for us to go down to the celebration party in progress in the hotel bar and tell everybody that we have rethought this, and the TV series thing is just something we don't actually have any interest in? But, tell you what, just to show you we are really not such bad guys we will buy the next round of drinks. That's diplomatic enough. Shouldn't be any hard feelings about that!" We laughed so hard it was hard to breathe. In summing it up, we concluded that although the concert footage was great, the rest of the pilot was so fucking lame it wouldn't get picked up anyway. So let them have their party downstairs and we just wouldn't worry about it anymore, since there was no way this thing would get picked up, hallelujah!

✳ ✳ ✳

Back in LA I went back to school, and Jan who was still on a medical leave of absence from his med school, was working on our musical stuff. We were a few months away from completing our contractual obligations to Liberty Records. We were considering having our own record label, Jan & Dean Records, to be distributed by our old manager Lou Adler's new record label, Dunhill Records. Now this was exciting.

Jan had just bought his first new home. It was a custom-built five bedroom house, plus a maid's bedroom. There was a huge living room with a spectacular round fireplace right in the middle of the room, a large spacious kitchen, and a beautiful big yard with a pool. This home was in a new expensive development called Bel Air Knoll, just west of the old Bel Air where Jan's parents lived. The house had a spectacular view of West Los Angeles, and overlooked a beautiful golf course that was still under construction.

Jan and his longtime girlfriend, Jill Gibson, were finally going to officially live together. Though they had seemed so excited for this, they had only been in the house for a couple of months before Jill abruptly moved out. Jan then asked me if I wanted to be his roommate, since I was still living at home with my parents. Sounded okay to me, especially if I could have the bedroom right next to the pool. He said, "No problem."

Jan was aware that I had tons of antiques and lots of framed artwork and photographs, and he seemed pleased that I was willing to bring all of that with me. This was an awesome situation for both of us. I was at school every day so I would see Jan in the morning, but I was gone all day. A couple of nights a week I had late classes so I didn't actually see Jan that much during the week. But we would pal around or do concerts on weekends.

Jan finally made some comment about why Jill had moved out. He said something about how Jill had caught him having sex with two girls he had snuck into the house late one night while he thought Jill was sleeping. I thought he was just kidding—after all who in their right mind would try to pull off something as risky as that. Surely not even Jan Berry would try that.

One day Jan calls me out to the pool. He had just gotten the lightweight cast off, and he was soaking his leg. There was still some pain when he walked, but it was getting better. He started to tell me about a guy he had met when he was in the hospital out in Chatsworth where he had spent a couple of weeks right after the train wreck. This guy had just kind of showed up at the hospital as a concerned fan, but was quickly recruited by Jan to be his personal gopher—you know, go for this and go for that. Mostly this guy snuck food and candy into Jan's room.

"Well guess what, Dean? This guy, Fred, just inherited millions of dollars and he wants to buy the house next door and be our neighbor."

"Hmmm, sounds charming! Go on."

Jan said he had called the developer that had built his house and the guy said that if Fred bought the "spec" house next door, Jan would receive a healthy commission. Then Jan went on to say Fred was a helicopter pilot and with his newfound wealth was considering buying his very own helicopter. Jan said he and Fred had visited the fire station right down the street on Mulholland, and they had a helipad and he and Fred were looking into the feasibility of being able to keep Fred's helicopter there.

And what would Jan get out of this? Well, Fred offered to fly Jan to med school every day. The hospital had a helipad. Jan pointed out that to commute to school and park would take over an hour. But by helicopter he could be at school in ten to fifteen minutes. Fred also wanted to fly us to concerts. Oh, and check this out, Fred would be very interested in investing a large sum of money in our record company. I was stunned. I thought Dunhill was putting up the cash to be our partner.

Who the hell is this Fred person? It was too weird. As I am trying to figure out a response to all of this, a helicopter arrives and lands in the golf course, not more than fifty yards from Jan's house. Christ almighty! Is that legal? Jan is stoked. A few minutes later, this skinny, nerdy looking guy gets out of the helicopter and joins us by the pool.

"Dean this is Fred Marx," says Jan. Within a few minutes Fred has talked me into riding in his helicopter. I had never been in one, so even though I thought he was a wee bit strange, I was intrigued. So off we went. And it was awesome. We followed the San Diego Freeway south until we found Sunset, then we turned east. I pointed out to Fred Dead Man's Curve, the spot where I used to park and make out with Cindy, Elvis's football field, and Jane Mansfield's house with the heart-shaped pool. We also spotted Brian Wilson's house, Doris Day's house, and Dennis Wilson's house. Then we turned southwest and flew over Twentieth Century Fox's backlot where we used to play as kids. After that we buzzed by my parents' house, then flew back to Jan's house and landed on the golf course again. He dropped me off and then flew away. I was running late for school so I hit the road. I guess I should have let Fred drop me off at school. Well, maybe next time.

The next weekend we were heading out for our first little mini-tour since Jan had broken his leg. The first concert was in Chattanooga, TN, the second was in Cincinnati, OH, then on to Virginia Beach, VA, followed by Cochran, GA, Tampa, FL, Orlando, FL, Montgomery, AL, Birmingham, AL, Atlanta, GA, Portland, OR, Hollywood Bowl, St. Louis, MO, Dayton, OH, Kansas City, MO. The last concert was for KOMA Radio in Oklahoma City and the master of ceremonies was the number one disc jockey, Charlie Tuna. We played two outdoor shows at The Wedgewood Village Amusement Park. The concert came off great, but little did we know that that would be our last concert for almost thirteen years.

On the plane ride back to Los Angeles, Jan informs me that Fred has committed a half a million to buy into the Jan & Dean record company. This would buy him 50 percent of the company, and Jan, because he would run the company, was taking the other 50 percent. Now it is true I was going to school at USC, but I still knew that 50 percent plus 50 percent made 100 percent. Hmm. Let's see, Jan & Dean Records. Jan owns 50 percent, Fred owns 50 percent. Dean owns . . . ?

"I must have missed something, so run that by me again," I said.

"Look," Jan said, "you will not only get a very nice royalty, three to four times what you get now, but we will also pay you a very healthy guaranteed monthly salary as well. This way you don't take any of the risk and we do. We could lose it all, and you would still have your money. That's not a bad deal." I was very surprised by this, but maybe I should have expected it. After thinking about it, it wasn't all that bad. However, I knew there was no way I would not negotiate some sort of percentage. I did have pretty good leverage. Jan & Dean Records carried a lot more credibility than Jan & Fred Records. I decided to just wait it out.

A few days later, I was getting ready to go to school when Fred pulled up to the house in a new Porsche. He said he was in the process of buying the house next door, a very similar house to Jan's. He said he had a key and would I like to walk through it and maybe give him some decorating tips. I said, "Sure, Fred."

As we walked through his house—after all he had a key—he explained that Jan's girlfriend, Jill, had offered to help him buy all of the furniture he needed since she had a decorator's license. I told him that I liked the house but that I had to hit the road or I would be late for school. He thanked me for taking the time to look and said, "Oh, say Dean, I left my apartment without my wallet. Could you loan me ten dollars until tomorrow?" I gave it to him and left. So let's see, when Fred buys the house, Jan will get a big commission check. Jan will also get a half a million dollars from Fred to be a partner in the record company. Jill was also getting a commission from ordering enough furniture to fill a big home. While driving to school I wondered if I would ever see my ten bucks again.

A few more days passed. On this particular morning I was once again getting my stuff ready to go to school when I heard Jan speaking very agitatedly to someone on the telephone. He sounded pissed. He hung up as I came into the room. "What's going on?" I asked.

"You won't believe this!" he said. "A few days ago Fred asked me if he could charge some clothes on my credit card because we have a big Jan & Dean Record Company business meeting with Lou Adler at Dunhill Records, and Fred didn't have any appropriate clothing. I said, sure go for it. So I get this bill this morning. He not only bought a lot of clothing, but he also bought some very expensive picnic baskets, one for his ex-wife and one for his girlfriend. He also bought a lot of non-clothing stuff. So I just called the bank where Fred said his money is being transferred to and they have never fuckin' heard of him. Then I called his alleged business manager, and he has never heard of him either! He's some kind of fucking psycho nutjob."

"Unbelievable, Jan. I'm really sorry about that."

On my ride to school I mused about the big house with the pool, the Porsche, the helicopter, Jan & Fred Records, all of the expensive furniture Jill had ordered and will apparently have to return, and all of the expensive items charged to Jan's credit card—but I was not at all amused about my ten dollars.

9

DEAD MAN'S CURVE

{1966}

I didn't see Jan that night, but I did see him the next morning. He was still agitated, so I asked him what the outcome of the Fred debacle was.

"Forget Fred. Look at this shit," he says as he hands me a document. Holy shit, it's a draft notice. "What fucking buffoons. I have a medical school deferment. I have a letter dated yesterday, April 11, from the California College of Medicine, that I will be readmitted in September. Plus I can barely walk—I still have screws in my bones and they want to draft me? This is bullshit! I have a business lunch in Beverly Hills, but I'll have to stop in the selective service office in Westwood Village and get this straightened out. This is outrageous."

With that he hobbled out the door, got in his new Stingray and quickly drove away. I packed up my stuff, got in my Stingray, and headed to school. I had one morning class and two afternoon classes, and I was to meet Jan at the recording studio that night. During my lunch break, I was sitting on the lawn eating my lunch in front of the library just across from the statue of Tommy Troja, when a classmate approached me with a concerned look on his face and asked me how Jan was doing. I wondered how he knew about

Jan's draft board notice, but then realized he was probably talking about his broken leg. I told him he seemed to be healing up pretty well, and he should be back to normal in a few months. He said no, I am talking about the car wreck he had this morning in Beverly Hills—it sounded pretty serious.

I was stunned. I asked if he was sure it was Jan Berry that he was talking about, and he said yes, and that they actually played one of our songs on the newscast. I grabbed my stuff and headed to a payphone to call Lou's office to see if this was at all true, and unfortunately it was true. Nobody seemed to know many details. Lou had headed to the UCLA hospital to find out the extent of his injuries; all we knew was that his injuries were serious. I just remember thinking this wasn't supposed to happen to him. For the most part he was always so lucky, like the cat with nine lives, always landing on his feet. I called his parents at their home, but they were at the hospital, so I got in my car and drove to the UCLA hospital.

The hospital was a blur. I didn't see any of Jan's family (they were in his room), but I did find Lou and he filled me in. It wasn't good—Jan was in a coma and undergoing surgery. I just really couldn't believe what I was hearing. Dennis Wilson and I had raced each other from one end of Sunset to the other a bunch of times and never as much as dented a fender, while Jan totals his Stingray on Whittier Drive, a residential street just off of Sunset and is having major brain surgery. They are not sure he will survive.

I left the hospital and started driving north toward Malibu. It was a dark night, but I could still see some light reflections glistening off the rolling waves. I rolled down the window to catch some ocean breezes, and I was very aware that my life from this moment forward was going to be forever changed, and obviously so was Jan's. Yes, I knew it wouldn't last forever, and I was truly grateful for the seven-year run we had. It had been magical to say the least. But this was not the ending I had envisioned.

A few days later I visited Jan with his parents. We could barely see him through all the bandages and medical equipment attached to him. He was semicomatose, but he was alive, and we were grateful for that. His mom sat on his bed and talked to him. She told him how much she loved him and that all of his many friends were all praying for his recovery, so not to give up. The doctors encouraged us to keep talking to him because they said he would hear us. When we left, I told his parents that I would move my stuff out of the house over the next few days. They said I could stay as long as I wanted, but one of Jan's younger brothers was going to house-sit until they figured out what to do with the house. It was pretty obvious that Jan would not be returning to his house anytime soon.

A day or two later, I went back to visit Jan. While I was there a doctor arrived. He tested to see if Jan was feeling any stimulation on both sides of his face, both arms, and both legs. As I remember, he felt some stimulation to the right side of his face, but nothing on the left side. He seemed to feel some stimulation on his left arm and leg, but really nothing on his right side. It was pretty obvious that the trauma to his head had been significant. The doctor said that Jan would have permanent brain damage, but they wouldn't know to what extent until the swelling of the brain diminished. It was going to be a long recovery, if he recovered at all.

Over the next few days I started moving my stuff out of Jan's house and back into my parents' house. I never minded living at my parents' house, and they enjoyed having me home again. My last day of packing up my things at Jan's, I went to the garage for something, and I was shocked to see Jan's totaled Stingray just sitting there. It literally looked like it had been dropped out of an airplane. I remember staring at the passenger seat, a seat I had sat in a lot. It was obliterated. The right side of the car was so badly damaged, a passenger would have been killed. On the other hand, the driver's side wasn't nearly as bad. I noticed that the seatbelt had been cut, so he must have been buckled up, but only across the lap, since this was before shoulder restraints. The steering wheel didn't look bent at all. What was noticeable was that a chrome windshield molding around the top inside of the windshield had popped loose and must have hit him in the head as the top half of his body lurched forward from the impact. I remember thinking that if he had been wearing a racing shoulder harness like I had in all of my cars, his head probably would not have come in contact with that molding.

I turned off the light, closed the garage door, and got in my 427 Stingray. I buckled my shoulder harness tight as I always did and drove home.

Meanwhile our opportunistic record company decided to take full advantage of all the press Jan was getting since the accident. I heard that they were going to release our remake of "Norwegian Wood," a song that the Beatles had just sold a bazillon records of. I needed to derail this somehow. I called them and pleaded for them to let me at least pick out the B side, and they begrudgingly said okay. Jan and I had always liked our recording of a song titled "Popsicle" from our *Drag City* album. It had never been released as a single. It was an up-tempo Jan & Dean classic, the total opposite of "Norwegian Wood." "Norwegian Wood" seemed dark to me, especially under these particular circumstances. I also requested studio time to remix "Popsicle" since it was already three years old. With the new technology that had become available, I could make the recording sound even better. They said okay, but I was on a strict budget.

April 22, ten days after Jan's accident, I showed up at United Recording Studios to remix "Popsicle." They called me into the office to remind me not to go over budget or they would call the record company. We had cut a lot of hits at that studio and they were treating me like I had just walked in off the street. I said I understood and headed to my studio. As I passed by studio A, the big studio, I looked in just to see if any friends were there, and I came face to face with Fred Marx, the guy that bamboozled Jan out of all that money by pretending to be a millionaire. It seemed he was up to his old tricks. Maybe he figured that nobody but Jan knew he didn't have a penny to his name, and since Jan was in the hospital he was in the clear. I am pretty sure he thought I didn't know about his scam. I asked him what he was doing there. He said he was recording a song he wrote. I looked into the studio and it was full of musicians including a string section. I smiled and said good luck and headed to my little studio. Well now, the office treated me like a stranger and they let Fred walk in off the street and spend about a hundred times what I was spending without making a fuss. Had they treated me with a little more respect I would have given them a heads-up, but they didn't, so I didn't say anything.

About ten days later, at my request, my pals in the mailroom called to tell me that the promotional records had arrived, and they had been instructed to stamp a star on the "Norwegian Wood" side of the record since that was the side the record company wanted played. I said that I would be right over. They gave me maybe a hundred records. I waited until they went to lunch, so I wouldn't get them in trouble, and started putting a star on the "Popsicle" side. I made up my own mailing labels, put them on the envelopes, and ran them through the stamp machine. Now the disc jockeys would get two records with different instructions, so they would have to listen and make their own decision. The following day I repeated what I had done the day before. And the next day I did it again. "Popsicle" hit number twenty-one on the Billboard charts and was number five in Canada. Need I say more?

10

MY SOLO FLIGHT: KITTYHAWK GRAPHICS

{1967–1979}

I was very happy to be settled into my new office on Sunset Boulevard. It consisted of three small rooms plus a bathroom and it also had a fireplace. The building itself was a very large old three-story Victorian estate built in the late 1800s. It had once been inhabited by President Taft. His granddaughter, Sarah Taft, now in her eighties, owned the building and lived in the penthouse suite on the top floor. The comedian Stan Freeburg had an office in the building as well as my old photographer buddy Ken Kim, who had a big beautiful office suite in what had once been the ballroom on the top floor. On the first floor was a marketing and design company owned by the older brother of an old high school buddy. This was a very creative community holed up in this beautiful old Victorian house—and it was now my time to be graphically creative.

As a recording artist, I was always frustrated by the almost total lack of attention given to the importance of music packaging, the total lack of knowledge concerning any branding of a recording artist, and the total lack of continuity. The A&R department didn't know what the art department was doing, the art department didn't know what the promotion department was doing, and they, in turn, didn't know what the public relations department was doing. None of them seemed to talk together, so nothing seemed to fit together. I was told many times to stay out of the art department. They would say to me, you make the music and we will make the art. Then I would ask the simple question—if you don't know what the music is about, how can you conceptually create the art? Well most of these guys were left over from the fifties. They were used to doing Julie London album covers, a headshot, a solid color background, and some type set.

Lou, Jan, and I had forced the art department to let us take professional pictures on the beach with a cool woody and some colorful surfboards for our *Surf City* album cover. We forced them to let us take some professional pictures at San Fernando Drag Strip for our *Drag City* album cover too. But if artists didn't know how to go about demanding this attention to detail to their branding objectives, it was not going to happen organically. You had to get really aggressive or it wouldn't happen—and the artist's career would suffer the consequences. And for some, they only got one chance to get it right.

My mission statement was for me to be the liaison between the recording artist and the art department. I was an advocate for the recording artist and his or her management team. The recording artist and the management team were the alpha dogs, and the art department was the tail. Hey, let's try it out!

So I needed a name. This was my first solo flight so I came up with the name Kittyhawk, named after the place where the Wright Brothers first flew in Kitty Hawk, North Carolina. I started by designing my first Kittyhawk Graphics project, my own logo, since I was the only one who would hire me. Then I designed my first business card, letterhead, envelopes, and invoices. I used old aeronautical themes for my designs, and I even dressed up in an old flying outfit for my first art directed photography session. The picture was then incorporated into my logo. Now that I had my own business card, I was finally underway to develop my new career. Jan & Dean were now in the rearview mirror.

My first big break came when I ran into an old music business friend who co-owned the record company that The Turtles were on. They were hot—"Happy Together" was a number one record at the time, and the company was compiling their first golden hits album. I was brought on board to execute a complicated design concept that The Turtles had envisioned. I also designed all the promotional items to accompany the marketing of the album including a poster, trade ads, t-shirts, and postcards. This was a very tough album cover to pull off, especially for me, since this was the first album cover from start to finish to come out of my graphic design studio. It was a real struggle, but in the end we were all pleased with the final product.

With the success of this first project, my old friends The Beach Boys hired me to design a trade ad for their next single release after "Good Vibrations," a very cool song titled "Heroes and Villains." The design ended up looking a lot like the *Sgt. Pepper* album cover, which came out a few years later.

One day I was visiting a lady I was dating who had been in the folk music group, The New Christy Minstrels. She and the only other girl in that singing group had broken away to form a duo. They shared a house up in Beachwood Canyon just under the famous Hollywood sign; many musicians lived in that canyon. One day a young guy shows up at the girls' front door. He is invited in and is introduced to me as Jim Guercio, bass player for the duo Chad and Jeremy, who had a hit record high on the charts at the time and were signed to Columbia Records. Jim informs me that he is the guy that wrote and produced their newest hit record, "Distant Shores," and that he has also formed a management company to handle Chad and Jeremy. My friend Jackie had shown Jim a Jan & Dean concert book that I had designed. He said he really liked it and he wanted me to design a concert book for Chad and Jeremy. We made an appointment for the next day at my design studio. Jim was blown away when he showed up at my office. Not only did he love the building—he loved my office, the furnishings, and decor as well. He especially loved my antique Coca-Cola Tiffany lamp shade hanging over my drawing table, my old oak rolltop desk, the matching oak filing cabinets, and all my antique accent pieces, including my vast collection of Coca-Cola trays.

We worked together for months on the Chad and Jeremy concert book, and we really enjoyed working together. I finally got the souvenir concert book finished and printed, and it looked awesome. Jim had me also design some business cards and stationary for his management company. Jim loved the offices so much that he asked me to ask the landlady if he could move into his own office there if a space ever became available.

Everything was going oh so smoothly until one day Jim arrives at studio with some very bad news. Chad and Jeremy had broken up. What were we going to do with ten thousand full-color concert books now? (I still have a few boxes in my storage unit.) We were both devastated. This was very bad news indeed. But because Clive Davis, the president of Columbia Records, had recognized Jim's immense talent, he had made Jim a staff producer at Columbia Records with a very nice salary and some advanced seed money to finance his own production company. So now Jim needed a real office.

Some office space had just opened up across the hall from my original design production studio. Jim moved in, and soon thereafter he was given his first assignment by Columbia Records. They had just signed a young group of guys from Chicago named The Buckinghams, so Jim asked me to start working on a concept for the album cover for this new group. Jim had liked a daguerreotype photo I had in my office of a Civil War Union soldier in his uniform. Jim asked me if it was possible to recreate something like that, and I said why not. An old friend of mine, Guy Webster, was emerging as the new photographer for up-and-coming rock stars. I had introduced him to our old producer and manager Lou Adler who needed some photography for his new group The Mamas & the Papas. The Guy Webster photos of The Mamas & the Papas really kick-started his rock and roll photo career.

Jim and I arranged a photo session with Guy to photograph The Buckinghams in both Union and Confederate Civil War uniforms. The pictures were amazing. We used the photos not only for the album cover but also for the sheet music, press kits, and some beautiful large posters. The Buckinghams' "Time and Charges" album went gold. They had four top 10 singles in a row. We now had it all really going—we were a great team. The continuity I was always pushing for was in full bloom with this particular project.

But then Jim arrived at our offices and informed me that The Buckinghams had fired him. They wanted to make their own decisions and felt they didn't need his input anymore. We were both very disappointed, to say the least, but within a few days Jim was given his next assignment. He was asked to produce a group that had done one album already but needed a real breakthrough project. The name of this group was Blood, Sweat & Tears. Jim had decided to just concentrate on the music this time and let them do all the rest of the creative work since they probably wouldn't appreciate anything we did anyway. And he was right. After a hugely successful second album that included at least three top 10 records, they too gave him the boot. At least it wasn't a Union or a Confederate boot, more of a wimpy little New York pointy-toed boot.

✳ ✳ ✳

Jim and I met in my ballroom studio one night to figure out what he should do next. He said he had a new plan in mind. From now on he would only work with groups that he discovered personally. That way he would own the name, the music, the publishing rights, and the management. I suggested that we should design a logo for the groups, which was something that I had always wanted to do. My inspiration was a few album covers that Peter, Paul and Mary had. The type font they used for their names was very stylized and it appeared on at least two album covers that I knew of and probably more. The same stylized type was used in all their printed promotional material, too, and I had actually seen just the three letters PPM in that stylized type. You knew what it meant, and that to me was branding at its finest.

We both realized that just the logo could dominate an album cover, preventing individuals from becoming bigger than the name. The name would then become the brand. If an individual got out of control, he or she could hit the road and nobody would know the difference. Then a replacement could be inserted and the musical entity would keep rolling on. The analogy I liked to use at the time was that when Anheuser and Busch passed away, did Budweiser disappear? Obviously not. So why couldn't a musical entity be designed around a particular unique, stylized music formula and be controlled by just one person. Then that same person could also control the visual component associated with the music by utilizing a prominent logo rather than the normal photographs of the individuals. This would make the visual more corporate and less personal.

Jim said he was flying to Chicago the next morning, and he was hoping to sign at least two musical groups that he had been following. He was so confident that he was going to sign them to a contract that he said I should start thinking about designing logos for both groups. Jim told me the first group is called Chicago Transit Authority, and the second group is Illinois Speed Press. Jim wanted me to start on the Chicago Transit Authority logo first. He would be out of town for at least two to three weeks but would call me when he actually got the contracts signed.

So the next day I started thinking about this logo for Chicago Transit Authority. While it was a very cool name, it had a lot of letters—twenty-three to be exact. Not many effective logos are a bunch of letters. Looking around my office I spotted not only my Coca-Cola Tiffany lampshade but also my big Coca-Cola drugstore button on the wall. We had included the Coca-Cola logo in the Chad and Jeremy concert book because Jim and I had always appreciated it and all its clever branding components. Looking at my Coca-Cola button, which was almost four feet in diameter, I thought maybe something like the Coca-Cola lettering style for the Chicago Transit Authority could work. The C in Coca-Cola could work very well for the C in Chicago, so I decided that's where I would start the design. I took a piece of tracing paper and put it over the "C" on my Coca-Cola button. I also traced the lower case "o" and the lower case "a." Then from there I tried to formulate the rest of the lettering.

A few days later Jim called to tell me that he had signed both groups. Then he asked me for a favor. He said the guys in the band were getting ready to drive from Chicago to Hollywood and they would need a house to live in while they recorded their first album. There would be at least ten people in all, traveling in a VW bus, so he would need a house big enough to hold at least ten people. He also asked me if I could find them a part-time gig playing at night somewhere locally. I told him I would gladly work on this for him. Meanwhile, it was back to work on the logo.

I worked day and night on that logo. Compared to the Coca-Cola logo, mine look like shit. I kept working on it, but it never got any better. There were just way too many letters. Coca-Cola was only eight letters—it had two Cs, two Os, two As, and one L. The designer only had to design four letters. And the letters had continuity, mostly all the same size. Chicago Transit Authority was twenty-three letters. I couldn't think of any other logo that incorporated twenty-three letters. I was very disappointed that it wasn't working out, and I realized that if Jim came back and I didn't have the logo done, he would be forced to hand over the design project to the Columbia Records art department. Once they had control of it I would be out of the loop. I also realized that hand lettering was a real art form and I was still a rookie designer.

When Jim did get back from his trip to Chicago I had some good news and some bad news. The good news was that I had found a house in Hollywood that was close to our offices. And I had also found them a beer bar called The Itchy Foot Mose that they could play at five nights a week and have all the free burgers they could eat—and these were not just any burgers. These were the world-famous Tardino Brothers burgers, as thick as they were juicy.

The bad news was that the logo was not finished and that I had taken it as far as I could. Jim looked over my rough drawings and he agreed that we were on the right track. The big Coca-Cola "C" was perfect, the lowercase "h" inside the "C" worked well, and the lowercase "i" dotted by the top of the "C" was also very cool. But the rest of it was not working. I was starting to realize that hand lettering was indeed a very complicated art form, not easily mastered overnight. Jim toyed with the idea of shortening the name to CTA, kind of like Peter, Paul and Mary's PPM. Okay, I could handle three letters. Going from twenty-three to three sounded great to me. After trying some possibilities, we just never came up with anything that was as good as all three of the words together. The upper and lower case gave it the Coca-Cola look, while three capital letters were not as interesting. This was my last chance to be involved with the logo, and it was now very obvious that it was going elsewhere. I could feel the logo slipping through my ink-stained fingers.

The next day the landlord of the house we were going to rent for the boys informed us that the house was not going to be ready by the time they arrived. We needed to find a place for the group to stay for at least three or four days. Jim and I thought if we combined our offices that the boys could sleep on the floor in their sleeping bags until the house was ready. The only problem was that we would have to ask our ultraconservative eighty-year-old landlady if a bunch of longhaired hippie rock musicians could sleep on the floors of our offices for a few days. Man, believe it or not, she said okay. A few days later the hippie van pulled up in our driveway on the corner of Sunset and Ogden and the boys piled out and moved into our two offices. They were all super guys—good-looking, masculine, and once I heard them play I knew Jim had a winner. We had some great times hanging out together with lots of beer, burgers, and late-night rock 'n' roll music at the Mose. It was a real fun time with lots of great memories.

Jim produced a great debut album. The logo designed by John Berg's New York-based Columbia Records art department was beautifully done. A few months later Jim dropped by my studio and said he wanted to run an idea by me. He was getting ready to start on the follow-up album, and he was still thinking about shortening the group's name. Well, I wish he had thought of that three or four months earlier, but better late than never. He really liked the word "Chicago" all by itself. It had a much better visual balance. The second album carried only the word Chicago on the cover, and now the logo could even fit on the record label and lots of other places the old one couldn't have. What a brilliant idea Jimmy G. If only he had thought of it in the first place, maybe I could have completed the logo myself—or maybe not.

✳ ✳ ✳

One day a tall, lanky, well-dressed guy with long hair and a full beard shows up at my office. He introduces himself as Bill McEuen. He is the producer and manager of a rock group newly signed to my old record company, Liberty Records, and he's looking for someone to design their logo, album package, trade ads, posters, promo pictures, and more. All right, that was great news, I knew I could beat anything they were turning out in the Liberty Records art department. Now if only the group had a simple name to work with, this could be a great project.

"So what's the name your group?" I asked Bill.

"The Nitty Gritty Dirt Band." Oh shit, whatever happened to good old names like Fabian, The Crows, The Who, War, Nilsson, Abba, Toto, and America? On the other hand it was one letter shorter than Chicago Transit Authority. Well, maybe I can talk him into shortening the name to The Dirt Band. Or maybe the title of the album is short—that would sure help.

"So Bill, what's the title?"

"Uncle Charlie and His Dog Teddy." Holy shit, that is more letters than Chicago Transit Authority. It's going to take two or three months just to do the lettering!

"Okay, but what about Woody Woodword and the Liberty Records art department?" I wanted to know. Bill said it wasn't a problem; he had negotiated his contract with the president of the record company so that he had full control over the music packaging, and he could deliver camera-ready art straight to the color separator without any interference from the art department whatsoever. This was the start of a brand-new era. The recording artist and his or her management team were gaining control over their own destinies, both musically and visually, and it was about time. I was positioned to be at the forefront of this new movement, so look out Woody!

Bill McEuen had an old black-and-white picture of his beloved uncle Charlie sitting in a rocking chair, holding his acoustic guitar with his sidekick at his feet, his dog Teddy. Uncle Charlie had been a big musical influence on Bill and his younger brother John McEuen, who was the Nitty Gritty Dirt Band's banjo, mandolin, and fiddle player. It seemed only right to do an album in his memory.

Conceptually we knew we wanted the primary colors to be earthy colors, like rich dirt brown. Once we were done, we took the artwork directly to the color separator, bypassing the art department altogether. A few days later we got the call to come look at the color proof. It wasn't the rich chocolate brown that the original art was. It was a kind of drab olive with tints of green and a little too much blue and yellow. We said please do it again, we want a warm rich chocolate brown. They said it was close enough, but we insisted. A couple of days later the new proof was ready. This one was purplish brown with too much red and blue. We wanted rich chocolate brown like a Hershey bar. They said it was close enough and we had better get used to it, but close enough wasn't going to work for us anymore. They were getting paid a lot more money than I was, and for that they needed to replicate the art that was given to them. That was their job! They called Woody at the art department to complain. Woody said he had seen the proof and it was close enough for him, but he had no say on this project; it was out of his hands. The color separators tried it again and this time it was perfect.

The next hurdle was the printer. We showed up at the Ivy Hill printing plant, which was totally unheard of at that time. Never before had the printing plant ever dealt directly with a recording artist representative. The printer foreman showed us the standard paper used for all album covers. We said we didn't like that paper— it was coated and slick. Because the cover art was a rich, earthy brown, it needed to look and feel like dirt, with a soft texture and a dull matte finish. Dirt is not shiny. We looked through the paper samples until we found exactly what we were looking for. That's it, right there! Print it on this handmade matte paper.

This created a new problem. They were used to gang-running album covers, sometimes four or five different covers all on one big sheet of paper, and none of the other companies would spend extra money on this more expensive paper. Our project would need to be on a single run all by itself, and this would be a lot more expensive. We loved the idea that this could be a single run. That way we could adjust the color to our own special needs. We said that's what we wanted and they agreed to call us when they were ready to print the run. A few days later we watched our beautiful cover run through the huge, five-color printing presses. It came out exactly like what we had hoped for.

The song "Mr. Bojangles" was released as a single and was a big hit. The album also did very well. One day Bill walks into my office and hands me a sheet of paper.

"What's this?" I asked.

"Just a Grammy nomination for the best album cover of the year," he said.

"No shit, you're kidding!"

"It's for real, so let's go to lunch and celebrate!" As it turned out, we didn't win the Grammy, but we were still honored to have been nominated.

The following year I was nominated again, this time for a cover I hated. As an interesting concept, it was fine, and it would have made a very interesting magazine illustration. But as a record album cover for an unknown band with no hit record, it made no sense. But my client wanted it, so I did it. The cover featured a chicken coming out of an egg with a gas mask on. The title of the album was *Pollution*. On the back of the album was the same chicken lying on his back looking very dead. Actually it had just passed out from the marijuana that had been blown in its face (not by me). The little chick was later revived, grew up to be nice and plump, and probably ended up in a cardboard box at Colonel Sanders.

The record stiffed, but guess what—the album cover won cover of the year. This was my first Grammy, and I was thrilled and embarrassed at the same time. I'd beat out some brilliant album cover designs that I should not have ever beaten out. The cover I thought would win the Grammy was "Sticky Fingers" by The Rolling Stones, but then there was "Bark" by Jefferson Airplane and "BS&T" by Blood, Sweat & Tears. "Polution" winning the Grammy was like Stewball winning The Kentucky Derby. Not that I was about to give the Grammy back. Well actually, I can't give it back. My daughters were playing "Grammy Awards" one night and they needed my Grammy for a prop. They set it down on a couch and sometime later they accidently sat on it and broke it into three pieces. So do I now have three Grammys? Well guess what, they misspelled my name on it anyway.

Over the next eight years I was nominated again, this time for *Dream* by the Nitty Gritty Dirt Band. I also got into the semi-finals five times for *Will the Circle be Unbroken* by the Nitty Gritty Dirt Band, *Love You* by The Beach Boys, *Gotta Take That One Last Ride* by Jan & Dean, and *Nilsson Sings Newman* and *The Point!* by Nilsson.

I ended up designing more than 150 album and CD covers throughout my career. Besides the Dirt Band, The Turtles, and Beach Boys, I also designed covers for Steve Martin, Harry Nilsson, Chicago, Michael Nesmith, Anne Murray, the Everly Brothers, Diana Ross, Linda Ronstadt, Canned Heat, Bobby Vee, and Dennis Wilson, just to name a few.

If you are interested in viewing some of my design work, you can find my Kittyhawk Graphics design portfolio by logging onto www.jananddean.com. You can also read some interesting stories about some of the other recording artists I worked with.

11
A MANSON ENCOUNTER

1969–1972

was also working on an album cover for another old pal, Mike Dasey, an extremely talented studio guitar player. He had independently produced a record and he wanted this project to be on his own record label, Hog Fat Records, and I was to design the album cover, the Hog Fat logo, and the record label. After many meetings at my Kittyhawk design studio, Mike needed me to bring some stuff to his house. He had a very eclectic house and furnishings. I remember falling in love with a metal Dobro guitar with an etched palm tree on the metal body of the guitar. This instrument had once been owned by Bobby Darin, and it was beautiful. Mike had something else he wanted to show off—an old Airstream house trailer that had been converted into a rolling recording studio.

"What's it for?" I wanted to know. He said he wanted to go on the road in search of people in remote places that were making ethnic or tribal music.

"Sounds like fun, Mike." Obviously he had too much money and too much time on his hands.

Then he offered me another job—a musical job. He had also created an instrumental album, full of rambling sitar music. The name of the group of studio musicians that had performed on this very odd recording was the Cylib People, whatever the hell that meant. He was asked by his record company to open for the Jefferson Airplane at the Shrine Auditorium in downtown LA on February 23 and 24, 1968. Mike in no way needed the money, but he needed some exposure to help him promote this new album. He had at least ten or so studio musicians who had played on the album, and he wanted all of them to play live on stage with him. He asked me to be a celebrity member of his group. Hell, why not? I thought.

But then again I didn't play any instrument very well, and he had some of the best musicians in LA—guys that had played on Beatles recordings, Bob Dylan records, Simon and Garfunkel, Elvis, Frank Sinatra, and more. So what would I play? Mike told me I would play percussion, wind chimes, finger cymbals, triangles, gourd, tambourine, and maracas. Damn, that sounded like fun. I told him to count me in. What a kick in the ass those two concerts were. The coolest part was that our group ended up making it onto an iconic Jefferson Airplane hippie poster (the one featuring a Native American) designed by the world-famous John Van Hamersveld.

A couple of weeks later Terry Melcher, the producer of Paul Revere and the Raiders and The Byrds, calls me to ask if I know anyone with a mobile recording studio. I told him I sure did. Terry tells me that Dennis Wilson of The Beach Boys has been pestering him to listen to his new friend's songs. Dennis had brought this bearded hippie guy up to Terry's house on Cielo Drive but he didn't have a guitar or cassette or anything. He had been expecting Terry to come out to his commune ranch way out in Simi Valley to hear his songs. Now Terry Melcher was not about to drive all the way out to some ranch to listen to a bunch of hippies, but he wanted to please his old buddy Dennis, so he offered to send someone out to the ranch to record them and then bring the tapes back to him for his evaluation.

I thought this was just what Mike Dasey was looking for, plus Mike had long hair, a full beard, and wore hippie garb, so he would fit in perfectly. I put Terry and Mike together and sometime later Mike calls me up and informs me that he is going out to the hippie ranch the following weekend and invites me to come along. I asked him to call me the following Friday to verify he was going for sure. He said he would do that. That Friday afternoon my new Malibu girlfriend, Cathy, called me up to tell me that the waves were awesome and I should come to her beach house and spend the weekend. So of course I forgot all about Mike and the hippies. I left work early that Friday to avoid traffic, and in the process, I missed Mike's call.

When I got into my studio on Monday morning there was a call on my answering machine from Mike saying he was still on for going to the hippie ranch the following day, Saturday, and if I was still interested to call him or meet him at his house Saturday morning. Oh shit, I had completely forgotten about Mike. I called to apologize. He was very excited so I asked him if he had discovered some great songs or maybe the next Grateful Dead.

"Jesus Christ Dean, you missed it, you really missed it. We had this groovy orgy with lots of beautiful young girls all wanting to please me."

"Okay, but what about the music for Terry?"

"Heeeey maaaan, we were getting the vibes together, I never got around to hearing any of their music. But I'm going back there next Saturday to record and then have another orgy. You got to come with me. It will blow your mind, plus blowing a few other things!"

"Okay I'm in, call me Friday to confirm."

On Friday my new girlfriend calls to tell me a bunch of our beach buddies have taken the day off to have a volleyball tournament at Zuma Beach. The weekends were always crowded, so playing on a Friday was a special opportunity, plus she had bought another new bikini. Man that Hog Fat Records logo would just have to wait till Monday. I was out of there.

Monday morning I get the message from Mike reminding me about Saturday. Oh shit, I forgot all about that hippie orgy thing again. I called Mike to once again apologize for not showing up. He said forget about it, so I asked how it went. He was quiet for a few seconds then he said he didn't want to talk about it. I asked if he recorded anything, but he said he didn't want to talk about it, so I dropped the subject. Now I was really curious about what had happened at the hippie ranch, so I called Terry but he hadn't heard from Mike yet. So then I decided to call a mutual friend, Errol Carmel, who was very tight with Mike. Errol said he wasn't supposed to tell anyone, but you know how that goes. He goes on to tell me this very scary story.

Mike arrived ready for work, smoked some weed with the hippies, and then they finally got around to singing some songs. After three or four songs Mike starts to realize that the songs they're performing are not very good, so he stops the tape recorders and offers some constructive criticism. With that, the short hippie leader with the long hair, full beard, and piercing dark eyes attacks him with a pitchfork. He knocks him down and has the pitchfork at his throat, screaming that he is going to kill him. Errol goes on to explain that the girls managed to talk the hippie leader out of killing him. Mike gets up, dusts himself off, gathers up just some of his recording equipment, and gets the hell out of there.

Mike was really shaken by the incident. Well so much for this peace and love, flower power bullshit—the dark side of the hippie movement was emerging. Jesus Christ, better not book these guys on *The Gong Show*, I thought. Then I started to realize how absolutely lucky I had been not to have been with Mike that day. I hope I would have come to his aid and not waited around to see if some drugged up hippie chicks would save him or not. Thank you volleyball, thank you Zuma Beach, thank you that new bikini! Mike never talked to me about what had happened to him. We eventually finished all of our projects, and the incident was soon forgotten.

Many months later, Los Angeles wakes up to the horrific news that Sharon Tate, Jay Sebring (who was my barber, by the way), and some of their friends were brutally murdered late that night at a home rented by Sharon Tate and her husband, Roman Polanski. The address was printed in the newspaper—it was on Cielo Drive in Beverly Hills. Holy shit, that was Terry Melcher's old house! I called Terry, and he was very shaken. The next night two more people were brutally murdered. We were all scared shitless.

A year or so goes by when the news breaks that people have been arrested for the Sharon Tate murders. They are a group of hippies led by a guy named Charles Manson. At the time of the murders they were all living in a commune at the Spawn Ranch in Simi Valley. Oh my God, this must have been the guy Dennis Wilson brought up to Terry's house on Cielo Drive last year and the same people Mike Dasey had a run-in with many months ago. Do you suppose Manson sent these people to the Cielo Drive house to pay back that rich kid Terry Melcher for ignoring their life-changing musical creations, not knowing that Terry had recently moved out? It would seem poor Sharon Tate and her friends were just in the wrong place at the wrong time.

Sometime later I ran into Mike Dasey. Gone was the long hair, gone was the beard, gone was the hippie wardrobe. He looked like a narc officer. He informs me that he has found Jesus and has written and is performing Christian music. He's also in the process of recording a Christian album. I wish him good luck. I never saw him again.

Meanwhile Terry Melcher gets into a motorcycle accident up at his weekend mountain cabin in Idlewild. He is taken to the hospital in Hemet, California, and the accident makes the evening news. A few days later Bruce Johnston and I drive out to the desert community of Hemet to visit Terry in the hospital. Terry was understandably shaken, but not about the accident. He showed us some letters he had gotten. Most were from fans and friends wishing him a speedy recovery, but some were not. He had also gotten death threats from the Manson Family. It was now pretty apparent that they were indeed specifically after Terry Melcher for some sort of convoluted revenge scenario that only they understood. It was very clear to me that the fifties and early sixties—the age of innocence—was indeed gone forever.

12

DEADMAN'S CURVE:
THE MOVIE

{1974–1979}

One day I get a call in my design studio from a guy named Paul Marantz. He introduces himself as a young lawyer working for the public defender's office in downtown Los Angeles. He also mentions that we are both USC Trojans. He goes on to tell me that many years ago, while he was still at USC, he had had a chance encounter with Jan Berry poolside at a hotel in Palm Springs. Paul, being a Jan & Dean fan, was intrigued by this chance encounter and the fact that nobody else hanging out around the pool knew or cared that this was Jan Berry. Paul sat with Jan for hour after hour listening to his fascinating story.

Paul, who dabbled in writing, started to realize there was a great story to be written about Jan & Dean and Jan's struggle to recover from his very serious injuries. Paul started to take notes, and this went on for two days until Paul had enough material for a very interesting article. He submitted it to the *Daily Trojan* where it was eventually published. Since then he had graduated from USC, passed the bar, and was now at the public defender's office. But he was bored to death. So recently he had decided to try some writing projects. He had reviewed some of his earlier writings looking for one to expand upon, and the one that jumped out at him was that Jan & Dean story. After he reread his article, he realized that some of the stories seemed to be inaccurate. Now understanding more about Jan's aphasia problems, he came to the conclusion that Jan had tried to be accurate but wasn't fully capable of recalling many events because of his brain damage. So that's why he was calling me.

He wanted me to read the old article, help edit it, and then help him expand on it to create a major article. I liked the idea, so we agreed to meet and start work on the project ASAP. We spent five or six months writing and rewriting the article in our spare time. By the time we finished the piece, the magazine that was the most interested in the article had gone belly-up. Paul then submitted it to everybody from *Esquire* magazine to *Playboy*. The consensus was that Paul's writing was very good, but it was felt that too much time had passed—more than eight years—and that nobody would remember or care about Jan & Dean anymore. (Well, the same thing could be said about this book!)

My feeling was that maybe that was true, but in my humble opinion, if the story was compelling enough, it didn't matter who Jan & Dean were. That argument fell on deaf ears. After Paul got turned down by all the current magazines, I suggested trying *Rolling Stone*. We submitted it to them and they loved it. Next thing I know, Annie Leibovitz shows up to photograph Jan & Dean for the cover of *Rolling Stone*. Jesus, can you imagine? Jan & Dean, ten years after their last major hit record, will be on the cover of *Rolling Stone*. How bizarre.

Paul and I rewrote parts of the story with a little more music and music industry flavor. It was finally ready to go to press, and guess what happens? Nixon quits and bumps us off the cover. We still got a full-page color picture and a great six-page article in the

September 12, 1974 issue, but now I started getting calls from Jan. He hates the picture they used. He complains that he has this grotesque, scary look on his face in the picture. Well Jan, I tried to explain, the only way they got that picture is that you must have made that face. If you don't want a silly face in a picture, then don't give them one to shoot.

Now Paul starts getting calls from people interested in making a movie about the lives of Jan & Dean. At one point Peter Fonda's production company was very interested. People were always telling me I looked a lot like Peter Fonda. I thought that was cool. Hey maybe I would get to meet Jane. Maybe she would get us mixed up and invite me over to dinner or something. That would be really cool as long as we didn't start talking politics. But nothing ever came of it.

The manuscript bounced around for a couple of years until it was submitted to CBS Television. They committed to paying for a screenplay, and if they liked the screenplay, they would make the movie. Paul and I were to meet with a lady screenwriter that CBS wanted to do the writing. I was doubtful of this woman's ability to write the screenplay for our movie. After all, what did she know about rock 'n' roll, surfing, and hot rods? Apparently nothing. The first draft of the screenplay was awful—it read more like a *General Hospital* soap opera script than a rock-and-roll movie.

I was devastated. This was the chance of a lifetime to have a movie made about us, and we were so close to getting this movie made, and now everything had been turned to shit. No way would CBS buy this totally lame screenplay. Well, guess again, they loved it! I couldn't figure out which was worse—to have the project scrapped, or to have it made in its present form. I was leaning a lot more toward getting the project back from CBS and waiting for a better deal. But our executive producer assured me that a director was being signed and that he would have the final say. If the director liked Paul's and my version of the film better than the screenplay, he could scrap the screenplay. But they couldn't proceed without my signature on the contract. Without knowing who the director was, I did not want to sign the contract. It was a classic catch-22. I agonized over it for quite some time until finally I was given an ultimatum: Sign the contract by Sunday night or the project will be shelved.

Ultimately I decided that I stood a good chance of retooling that lame screenplay, so I crossed my fingers and signed on the dotted line. The director was hired a few weeks later. His name was Richard Compton. He was about our age and had made a very cool TV movie called *The California Kid*. In the movie, the leading guy drove around in a great-looking hot rod with a very cool flame paint job. Hey, this Richard Compton is my kinda guy. He also thought the screenplay was trash. I pointed out to him that the film should be musically driven, while the original screenplay only featured three songs. Say what? When we finished the rewrite it now featured seventeen songs. Working with Richard Compton on the script was such a pleasure. Paul and I really lucked out getting him for our project. I was very pleased with the final draft of the screenplay.

Next came the hiring of the actors who would be playing our parts. Trying to find someone who looks and, if directed properly, acts like you was a bizarre concept for us. We all agreed that trying to get big-name guys might not work in our favor. The audience would never be able to think of these known actors as being Jan & Dean. Since the audience would need to be totally convinced by the characters of Jan and Dean, household names just wouldn't work. Whenever people asked who we were casting for our parts, I would tell them that it was down to Robert Redford or Steve McQueen for Jan, and Woody Allen, Don Knotts, or Richard Pryor for me. The consensus was that those were all really good choices—except for Woody Allen. That was a real stretch.

A final decision was eventually made. Two very talented and seasoned actors were chosen. Richard Hatch from *Battlestar Galactica* and *The Streets of San Francisco* was to play Jan's part. Bruce Davidson, the star of the movies *Willard* and *Short Eyes* was to play me. Although Richard Hatch was not blond like Jan, his facial features looked very similar to Jan's facial features. Bruce Davidson, on the other hand, very closely resembled me in appearance and coloring—somewhat closer than Richard Pryor.

I also suggested to Richard Compton that in the scenes where we are recreating playing live music on stage, we should use a real band and not actors. I had found just the right guys for the job, a group called Papa Doo Run Run. They specialized in playing Jan & Dean and Beach Boys music. They knew the songs backwards and forwards, and I felt it was important that even if "Surf City" was being lip-synched by the actors, the backup band should be playing all the right chords. It was a small thing, but why not do it right? Also they were good-looking guys, which couldn't hurt.

I was starting to realize that if this movie was a hit, there might be a chance for us to get the opportunity to play some live music once again. And if that happened, why not do it with Papa Doo Run Run? They were a successful, working tribute band with all the road equipment; plus they had a truck with a liftgate and a roadie to boot. I also started to realize that this movie would be like a two hour K-tel record commercial. We could potentially sell millions of albums, and maybe finally get our first platinum album.

I arranged a meeting with the new president of our old record company plus his staff. This staff included some old friends who were left over from when we were with the label. I had proposed a repackaging concept to them. Basically it was a golden hits package, eight top ten records, plus four bonus songs I had recorded for the movie soundtrack. I also suggested that the graphics should be modern and not look like an oldies package or a typical soundtrack.

I did remind them that I had gotten them two Grammy nominations for recording packaging. Those were the first and last Grammy nominations they ever got.

You would have thought I was speaking Swahili (which nowadays probably works just fine). The president of the record company gives me a lesson in record sales 101. One play on television is meaningless, he tells me with a straight face. Now mind you, this came from a guy that had just been fired for ineptness at another major record company. So why is he now running this one, nepotism? I went back to my office, and as soon as I got back one of my old friends who was in on the meeting called. He told me that as soon as I walked out the door, the president called the warehouse to see how many old Jan & Dean golden hits packages they had left in stock. They had eight or nine thousand, and he was pumped. He had a brilliant idea. He called the art department and told them to design a sticker that said "Music from the CBS TV movie *Deadman's Curve*." Man, he was on a roll. Now he could finally dump those pesky eight or nine thousand albums that had been sitting around collecting dust. This was indeed a great day.

EMI television and CBS were spending $1,400,000 on a TV movie of the week to air in primetime on Friday night, February 3, 1978, to up to 35 million people. United Artists Records (formerly Liberty Records) would pony up a mere $238 on 10,000 color stickers and move those eight or nine thousand dusty old LPs. Holy shit, they could net close to ten grand!

Now just to put this into some perspective, CBS's *Deadman's Curve* did end up getting a thirty-three share, which means there were more than 35 million viewers. NBC put out a very clever Monty Python spoof on the Beatles called *The Rutles*. Although it was a very funny movie, it was too "inside" and only people in the music business could appreciate the humor. Consequently it stiffed. It had less than one half the viewers we had. But the soundtrack, which didn't have a single hit record, ended up going gold—because it was Warner Bros. That means it made one million dollars or more in sales. So, Mr. One Play on Television Is Meaningless, what other pearls of wisdom can you share with us? You just cost Jan & Dean personally one million, maybe as much as two million in sales. I hope you're happy with your ten grand. Well, I guess there's a reason Warner Bros. Records is still very much in business while United Artist Records is no more than a bad memory. But back to the movie.

I had also written a scene in the movie for my old Beach Boy pals, Mike Love and Bruce Johnston. Soon after the first airing of *Deadman's Curve*, Mike Love called me at my design studio. He told me that before the movie, he was being asked about Jan & Dean maybe once a year, but immediately after the airing of the movie, he was being asked at least ten times a day. And at least half of these inquiries were from kids. Mike said I should seriously think about putting Jan & Dean back together again. Furthermore, if I wanted to witness this newfound interest in Jan & Dean for myself, he could arrange for us to accompany The Beach Boys on their next tour. He offered to make a special guest place for us in The Beach Boys music set. We would sing two or three Jan & Dean songs in the middle of their set, then we would return for the encore which included "Barbara Ann," which I sang lead on anyway.

I loved Mike's idea. It would be fun to hang with the guys again, just like the old days. I couldn't have been any happier. It was great to get at least one more chance to perform to a brand-new audience. It had ended so abruptly some twelve years earlier, and I had always regretted the fact that I hadn't known that the last concert we did just before Jan's accident was going to be the last one for a very long time. If I had known, I would have soaked up every minute of it. As it turned out, I remembered absolutely nothing about that night, and that was a shame.

✳   ✳   ✳

On an average day I would get to my studio between 10:30 and 11:00 a.m., answer my calls, go through my mail, do some book-keeping, and organize my day. Then I would run errands—pick up and deliver work to my suppliers, meet with clients, and eat lunch, usually at the Sunset Grill in the late afternoon. Then I would be back at the studio after my late lunch. That would be my time for settling in to design. I was normally there at my drawing board until midnight or later. Two nights a week I would go to the West Los Angeles YMCA to play indoor volleyball for three hours, grab a burger at the Apple Pan or a chili dog at Pinks, and then go back to my studio or go home. Friday night was date night and Saturdays I worked on my old, three-story English chalet built in 1924 that was once owned by Humphrey Bogart. I really liked my schedule, but I sensed that fooling around with music again could change my cozy routine big time.

The Beach Boys rehearsed our biggest three songs: "Surf City," "Little Old Lady from Pasadena," and "Dead Man's Curve." I went to one of the last rehearsals and I thought it sounded great. I was also working on the new tour t-shirt design. We called it "The Surfing Déjà Vu Tour." We were also having tour jackets made, uti-lizing The Beach Boys' neon logo design that I had designed for them a few years earlier. It was all coming together. I could barely wait for the limo to pick me up and take me to the charter part of the LA airport. When the day finally arrived, I felt so overwhelmed sitting in the back of a stretch limo, heading for a rendezvous with a chartered jet to do eight concerts with my good old friends The Beach Boys.

As I drove towards the airport, I shook my head as I tried to grasp what was happening to me. For the last twelve years my routine had been basically the same. I may have taken four or five four-day vacations in all that time. This was my life for the past twelve years, almost twice as long as my first Jan & Dean life, which had lasted seven years. So why was I in the back of this stretch limo on a weekday heading for the airport? What would Johnny Rivers think if he needs some new typeset for his press kit and I am not there to answer his call? Will Linda Ronstadt want her stuff back to give to someone else? Will Nilsson, Michael Nesmith, the Dirt Band, or Steve Martin wait for me? Screw them,—now I'm the one in the back of the limo on my way to a private charter jet— it's my turn now.

The limo pulls into the charter part of the airport, rounds the corner, and pulls up beside a beautiful white and blue jet. There are some photographers milling around the plane. Mike meets me by the stairs going up into the airplane. He introduces me to the photographers. One is from *People* magazine. Right about now I would normally be ordering a double chili cheese or an egg burger from Joe's Sunset Grill. Today someone from *People* magazine wants to photograph me boarding a chartered jet headed to Pittsburgh. This is awesome. The pictures are taken and it's time to board. I am dying to see what the inside of the charter jet looks like. Oh God, it was beautiful. It was set up more like a living room than an airplane with lots of wood paneling, beautiful custom seats, a plush carpet, and sexy lighting. There were two very attractive stewardesses who would cook special meals for everyone—maybe even a double chili cheese.

As we settled in, it became apparent that there were three camps inside the plane. Dennis Wilson and The Wild Bunch were in the front drinking, drooling over a stack of girlie magazines, or playing cards all the while busy plotting how to piss off Mike Love. Mike had surmised this and he had laid claim to a separate compartment in the back of the plane that could be closed off from the rest of the plane with a solid oak door. This is where the meditators were camped. It was very quiet in that part of the airplane, a polar opposite from the front of the plane. Somewhere in between were the neutral guys. The buffer zone, I called it Switzerland. Most of the members from Switzerland could make occasional trips into either one of the other camps, just to keep in touch. But the polar camps rarely visited each other.

Trying to stay neutral, I spent most of my time in the Switzerland camp with the big kahunas, Brian Wilson and Carl Wilson, Bruce Johnston, Alan Jardine, and Jan. There have been five or six books written trying to explain Brian Wilson, so I'm not going to try. That said, at one time he was a very gifted songwriter and a brilliant song arranger. He was also a very clever and funny guy, but since his emotional problems had come to the surface, he was nothing like the old Brian and that was truly a shame. My partner Jan was in this camp and he and Brian had a lot in common. Bruce Johnston spent most of his time in our camp along with most of the support staff. Carl Wilson tried to spend equal time in all three camps, and served as a kind of ambassador.

I was also one of a few that was accepted in any of the camps. Mike and I were old friends who spent time together occasionally, usually girl related. One time just the two of us drove his new GTO right down the middle of a near empty Harbor Freeway, hitting speeds of well over a 120 mph because there were snipers on the overpasses—this was during the Watts riots. Dennis and I, on the other hand, would go drag racing, go-kart racing, surfing, or sailing. I had just spent a week in Maui shooting pictures of Dennis to be used for the new album cover that I was designing for him. We surfed, took pictures, surfed, ate, took pictures, and surfed some more. We had a great time. I cared a lot for both Mike and Dennis and it pained me to see them spar with one another.

✳ ✳ ✳

The gig with The Beach Boys had the potential to be great. Huge
concerts, some of the best rock 'n' roll songs ever recorded to draw
from, lots of money, lots of chicks, and a chartered jet. It could
be paradise, but as you know by now nothing is ever that simple.
The flight was so much fun compared to a normal coast-to-coast
flight on a commercial jet and it seemed to go by much too quickly.
I wanted to soak up every minute of it. When we landed in Pittsburgh, we were met by five limos that took us to our hotel. Dennis
and I met in the hotel bar that night. After downing a six-pack he
threw up, so I went to bed.

The next day a big bus picked us up at the hotel and took us to
Three Rivers Stadium. There is a place on the freeway, just coming through a tunnel, where the stadium comes into full view. And
an awesome sight it is, especially if it's full of people, which it was.
From almost total oblivion to a packed stadium in just a couple of
months—I must be dreaming. Please don't wake me.

With the stadium now in sight, Carl Wilson walks up to my
seat, kneels down next to me, and asks, "Now 'Surf City' is in the
key of B flat right? But it starts out in A flat and then there is that
weird modulation at the end right?" Christ, what a strange time
to be asking me these questions . . . oh I get it, he's pulling my leg
or something. Three Rivers Stadium is looming up out the front
window, packed to the rafters (if it had rafters) and we were to be
on stage in three hours or so and the lead guitarist wants to know
what key to play "Surf City" in. That Carl, what a sense of humor.
Wait, holy shit, Carl doesn't have a sense of humor. But I thought
they had rehearsed our songs? I was sure that the time I went to
the rehearsal studio it sounded fine. Was Carl there or was that
Eddie Carter playing guitar? Now I can't remember.

Finally the big moment arrives. The Beach Boys hit the stage. That means Jan & Dean will be out there in another forty minutes or so. The minutes ticked off until it was our time to walk onto that monster stage. Mike did a very cool introduction and the audience gave us a huge ovation. What a great setup. The Beach Boys had the audience primed. We didn't have to say anything, all we had to do was walk out there. There were no expectations, we really couldn't lose.

The songs went by so fast. After the second song, I was feeling my oats. I stepped up to the microphone and asked 65,000 people if they wanted their picture in *People* magazine. Of course they did. So I asked Roxanne the photographer from *People* magazine to climb up on the drum riser. Then I explained to the audience that we would now turn around to face the camera and they were to wave at Roxanne, which they did. Roxanne snapped some pictures and we turned back around, did our last song, and went off. It was awesome, it couldn't get any better than this, could it? Oh yes it could. Fifteen minutes later, with the audience at a frenzied peak, we were called out again for the encore, "Barbara Ann," The Beach Boys big hit single, which I had sung lead on, and the closer for the encore, "Fun Fun Fun." These are possibly two of the greatest rock 'n' roll songs ever recorded. The stadium was rockin' and a rollin'.

All too soon, it was over. I will always cherish that very special afternoon and luckily I made sure to get the picture from *People* magazine documenting it. We went on to play eight more concerts. One of the last ones was the Omni in Atlanta. I noticed something profound. It all came about from the fact that The Beach Boys hated to get stuck in the traffic at the end of the concert. So there was a policy that you packed up all of your personal stuff before going on stage. It would then be loaded in the limos and the limos would be sitting right by the stage door, engines running. On stage we would finish singing "Fun Fun Fun," the last encore song, and the backup musicians would keep playing. We would wave goodbye, run down the stage stairs through the backstage and out stage door right into the waiting limos while the band continued to play. The audience would stay in place hoping that The Beach Boys would come back out just one more time. The music would still be playing, but that was just a ploy to keep them from heading for the parking lot. We were out of there before the music stopped.

Now to get to the profound part. I noticed that as I got into the limo I would still be singing my part in "Fun Fun Fun"—even as the limo pulled away. I was still singing or humming my part another five or ten minutes down the road. I was struck with the fact that I was still singing this song, even when I didn't need to. It was still fun to sing after all of these years.

The limos would pull up right to the stairs to the charter jet. I climbed up the stairs still wearing my sweaty stage shirt and the flight attendant would take my drink order, then my dinner order. By then our personal bags were brought aboard and we would then change out of our stage clothes and into our travel clothes.

At our very last concert, we were all backstage getting ready as usual. I now had a new job—hand printing out the music set list for the night, and making at least ten copies so everybody had one. This particular afternoon somebody wheeled in this little special needs person in a wheelchair into our green room. Someone yelled, hey it's Paula. With that Dennis spots her and runs over and attacks her. He pushes her over in her wheelchair and is on top of her hugging and pretend-French kissing her, and she is loving it. That became one of my fondest visual memories of Dennis Wilson. That alone should have gotten him into heaven.

On the last day on the flight home, I spent most of the time in the cockpit with the pilots, who even let me fly the plane for a while. This was one great adventure, a memory I shall keep forever. Thank you Mike, thank you Carl, thank you Alan, thank you

Bruce, thank you Brian, and thank you Dennis, wherever you are. Oh, and thank you *Deadman's Curve* the movie. Thank God it got made, or this awesome "Surfing Déjà Vu Tour" would have never happened.

13

BACK TO KITTYHAWK

{1979}

Back in my design studio the next day after coming off the road, I was thinking back to where I was just twenty-four hours ago. I was sitting in the copilot's seat of a charter jet buckled into my seat with gold-plated buckles. Flying cross-country, dipping down to get a better view of the Grand Canyon, pushing cool looking buttons, talking on the radio to people I didn't even know—and in just twenty-four hours I am back at my same old rolltop desk looking at the same old messages. Johnny Rivers is pissed off; the promotional flyer that I had designed and printed for him is not acceptable. The blue color of his eyes wasn't printed blue enough and he wants it reprinted, but now it's almost too late. Walter Egan, the "Magnet and Steel" artist, needs to add some last-minute credits to the back of his album cover. Steve Martin wants one of the lipstick marks on his new *Comedy Is Not Pretty!* album cover moved closer to his fly. The suits at Warner Bros. want the lipstick prints as far away from his fly as possible. My girlfriend, who provided the lipstick prints, wants them even further away from his fly than Warner Bros., and she's also worried her parents might find out.

Jesus Christ, I want to be back on that jet, back on stage at Three Rivers Stadium, back in some fancy hotel bar drinking tropical drinks singing doo-wop songs with my buddies and being hit on by more women than I could keep track of. And may I add, making more money in one night than I made in two to three weeks at my drawing table. In other words, one weekend of rock 'n' roll income equaled one month of graphic design income.

I realized I needed to rethink this graphic design stuff. I had entertained the possibility of giving the music thing another try, but now was the time to stop talking and either commit to it or forget it. With just one phone call I could commit to it—but there would be no turning back. I picked up the phone and made the call.

My first call was to a guy in New York who called me right after the first airing of *Deadman's Curve*. His name was Winston Simone. He was a Jan & Dean fan who was working for his very successful investment banker father with offices on Park Avenue. Winston's first love was music, so with his dad's blessings he was actively looking to get involved in the music industry. He was smart, ambitious, rich, and had a great sense of humor—sounded like my kind of guy.

We had entertained the possibility of going into partnership with the purpose of resurrecting the careers of Jan & Dean based on what Winston and I saw on The Beach Boys' tour. Plus the more the records were being played on the oldies stations, the more demand there was to hear the band in concert. The more the band played live, the bigger the following, the more the records sold, and so on. We sure saw that for ourselves on the Déjà Vu Tour. Jan & Dean still had recognition value, thanks to *Deadman's Curve*. We felt we could at the very least do very well playing live concerts. Then there was the merchandise to consider too, and if we got real lucky maybe even a new record deal.

But the live concert part of the business was our first order of business, and we needed a backup band. Traditionally a group of people get together and buy their own equipment, practice a bunch, and when they get good enough, they go out and play live. If they get lucky, a record deal comes along and they get their music played on the radio. Then their concert attendance is augmented by the amount of play they are getting on the radio. One business feeds off the other, and vice versa.

Jan & Dean didn't have a band, but we were getting a lot of play on the radio, even though we hadn't made a new record in fifteen years. Classic oldies stations were everywhere and they had big followings. Jan & Dean had five or six records in regular rotation on each and every classic oldies station all across the nation. That's more play then we got in the sixties with a huge hit, so now it was like having six or seven hits all at the same time, kinda like the Beatles plus some.

In the sixties, or even now if you have a hit record, you get maybe two to three months of play, then it's over. On the oldies circuit, the songs never die, though many of the artists have already gone on to the American Bandstand in the sky. But the songs are like the Energizer Bunny, they just keep going and going and going. So here we are getting a lot of play on the radio, getting songs used in movie soundtracks and in TV commercials, and we don't even have a band. This is ass-backwards as usual, so Winston wants to know what to do about a band. Our choices are to handpick some musicians and form a band from scratch, or find an existing band who has already gone through the learning curve of playing live. And hopefully they already own their own equipment and maybe even a truck, and we simply plug in Jan & Dean.

I liked the latter idea. It was a lot less work and would allow us to get up to speed a lot quicker with a lot less capital to invest. I reminded Winston that the group I used in *Deadman's Curve* was a group that specialized in playing Jan & Dean and Beach Boys music, and that was precisely why I wanted them to be in the movie. I didn't want the typical TV version of a rock 'n' roll band pretending to play an instrument. This band was featured in the movie, with lots of exposure twenty to thirty million imprints, so why not use them? Throw in the fact that they had named themselves after the opening line of the Jan & Dean song "The New Girl in School" ("papa do run day run day") and it might look like we had planned it all along (which actually I had).

My next call was to Papa Doo Run Run. I wasn't really sure if they would be interested, but it turned out that they were. I told them Winston would formulate the partnership and work it out with them. My next call was to my old pal Bruce Johnston. He and Terry Melcher had just signed a production company deal with RCA Records and they were looking for new artists. Bruce had a cameo part in *Deadman's Curve* and he had met Papa Doo Run Run on the set. I told Bruce about my impending career change and that I was looking for a record deal for Jan & Dean's new band. He said he was very interested. I thought it was important for Papa Doo Run Run to have some of their own credibility. Having a record on RCA Records with no overt Jan & Dean nepotism, produced by Bruce Johnston and Terry Melcher, would increase their perceived value from a garage band to the major leagues. This way they wouldn't seem like they were riding on Jan & Dean's Hawaiian shirttails.

I called Winston back and told him we now had a band, two roadies, equipment, and a truck, so Winston's next job was to find the right booking agent for us and start booking live concerts. We were underway. After I hung up the phone I thought, holy shit, what did I just do? I looked at the old Roy Rogers clock on my rolltop. I had just spent almost four hours on the phone on music related business. This was the most time I had spent on business unrelated to graphics in thirteen years. For a moment, it felt weird and I wanted to undo it all. I had a nice situation, my own small business, a sweet little design studio, no partners, a manageable roster of clients, no big surprises, and volleyball on Tuesdays and Thursdays. I was in a comfortable groove. I did basically the same thing every day, I had a very pleasant routine, why did I want to shake it up? Maybe I needed to go to the Sunset Grill, have an egg burger and a Dr Pepper, and think about what I had just done.

The next couple of months were a blur. Everything was happening so quickly. Jan and I flew up to San Jose, California, where Papa Doo Run Run were based. We rehearsed for a couple of days and then played our first official Jan & Dean headlining concert since Jan's accident. We were playing at the Santa Cruz Civic Auditorium and it came off great. By then we had selected a booking agent, and they were putting together a summer tour for us. It was shaping up to be ten times bigger than we had ever done before and making ten times the money we had ever made before.

Meanwhile, I was able to keep my graphics business going at the same time, just in case. I was putting the final touches on Steve Martin's *Comedy Is Not Pretty!* LP package. The color separator was going to have a color key made for me to look at in about a week or so. I remembered that we were going to be in North Carolina playing at a huge amusement park called Carowinds, so I asked the color separator to please FedEx the color key to me there and I would call them if I needed to make any changes.

The day we got to Carowinds, the color key was waiting for me. It looked great, even the lipstick marks were perfect. I called and told them to send it on to the printer and thanks for the great job. Later that day we played our first of two shows to a sold-out audience of close to ten thousand people.

Meanwhile, outside the amphitheater a young lady, a twenty-three-year-old junior executive at Anheuser-Busch named Susan

Vogelberger was strolling by the amphitheater with her college sweetheart. They had heard a lot of commotion going on inside the amphitheater and looked up at the marquee to see who was causing all of this ruckus. Wow, they must have thought, maybe it's Molly Hatchet on stage or could it be Cheap Trick, Joan Jett, or maybe Jefferson Starship? But no, it says Dan & Jean—no, wait, it says Jan & Dean. They look at one another, obviously thinking who the hell are they? Probably some teenybopper group. So they kept walking.

Backstage after the second sold-out show, the management, knowing we were staying in town because we had the next day off, invited us to be their special guests back at the park for Steve Martin's show. I had no idea Steve was playing there the following night. What a cool surprise. I told the management folks that Steve and I were old friends and that I would love to see his show. They said they were meeting his private jet at the general aviation airport in the morning, and would I like to go with them to pick him up? You bet I would. Then I remembered I had the color key of the new album cover. I bet he would be surprised to see it and me in North Carolina.

The next morning we drove to this little airport and twenty minutes later a little Learjet touches down and rolls right up to our car. I get out of the car, clutching the color key. Down comes the ramp and down the stairs comes Steve carrying a suitcase and his banjo case. I walked up to Steve as he hits the ground. He squints at me and seems totally confused.

"Dean, what are you doing here?" he asks.

I hold up the color key and say, "I thought you needed to see where the lipstick marks ended up." He still looked really confused. I really had him going. "Look where Warner Bros. made me move the lips. It really pisses me off so I thought you should see this right away." He is still baffled as to why I was there, out in the middle of nowhere, two thousand miles from my design studio talking about some lipstick marks that had been shifted a quarter of an inch. For thirteen years he had been coming to my design studio or I had brought stuff to him at his Laurel Canyon house. I was always within a mile radius Monday through Friday, and you could count on that. But now he found me here in North Carolina—what was going on?

We got in the car, and I was still keeping the bit going, although it was starting to get uncomfortably old. But by now I didn't know how to get out of it. Finally one of the guys from the park told Steve that Jan & Dean had played at the park the night before—two sold-out shows, by the way. I expected Steve to say all right Dean, congratulations, good for you, aha, you really had me going. Instead he said he didn't feel well and was looking forward to taking a nap.

Man this was weird and I realized that the balance of power had shifted. For thirteen years I had been his graphic designer and one of his biggest fans. I didn't know him in the prime days of Jan & Dean, when he would have been the wannabe, and we had been the guys with all those gold records and hanging with the Beatles and the Stones and Elvis and The Beach Boys. Now our career had come full circle and we were working the same big venues he was. But the big difference was that he had worked hard for fifteen years to get there. It took us just fifteen weeks from that call to Winston Simone. I took Steve's word that he just wasn't feeling well and left it at that. After all, he had always treated me like a friend and always seemed to appreciate the work that I gladly did for him. We dropped Steve off at his fancy hotel and I told him I hoped he would feel better after a nap. He put on a great show that night as usual, but still said he wasn't feeling well, so I said a quick good-bye, see you in LA. I was starting to realize that nothing was going to be the same as it had been. Change was inevitable—some for the better, some for the worse.

Back in LA things were still happening quickly, mostly all good stuff. We were getting offers to play some great dates, amusement parks, state and county fairs, big waterparks, big amphitheaters, and even some stadiums. It was now becoming apparent that I would not be able to hold on to my graphics business, so I informed my clients that I would finish all of our work in progress, but regretfully I would not be able to take on any new projects. I offered to introduce them to some of my most competent and creative graphic designer friends who would be more than happy to get their business.

I was also aware that my relationship with my girlfriend Cathy was going to be impacted. Now she would probably say "What relationship?" since we hardly saw each other, and she would be right, but in my mind I thought of it as a relationship. Nevertheless this was probably another change, even though it would be for the best, that was going to be difficult. I cared very much for her and her family, and I loved spending time with her at her beautiful Malibu beach house. But getting back into the music business was going to be a full-time job and I would be on the road much of the time, so trying to keep a relationship going was probably not a good idea. I needed to man up and be honest with her that I needed to let her go so she could move on and find a super guy that could give her a stable relationship. I make it sound like she would be brokenhearted, but quite honestly I think she was relieved. I know her parents were.

14

KICK ONE THROUGH THE UPRIGHTS SUMMER TOUR

{1980}

Now that I was all in, it was time to roll out the first official spring, summer, and fall music tour. We even gave the tour a name, "Kick One through the Uprights," and I designed the logo for it. This, by the way, was our first tour ever. I mean ever. Up until that point, we had only done one-off dates, a weekend here and there, and a few individual dates in between. And believe it or not, Jan & Dean had never been on a tour bus either—and that never changed. We flew everywhere, occasionally renting cars or a van to get to where we were going. So this yearlong tour was new territory for us. We started with an early spring date at Harrah's Casino in Lake Tahoe. This was the only venue that we would play for a week or maybe even two weeks at a time. Most everything else were one-nighters.

We had been at Harrah's for a couple of days when our boss called me into his office one night before our early show. He starts by telling me how much he likes us and how happy he is for all of us that we were doing such great business at Harrah's. But he tells me there's a problem. He's very concerned about what has been occurring late at night after our shows. He goes on to tell me that some of his plainclothes security officers had reported to him that Jan was wandering around the casino late at night looking to buy cocaine.

I was stunned. I had no idea that Jan did cocaine. Our boss said it was really none of his business unless it started to affect his performance. If it did, we would be fired. He just wanted to let me know how dangerous it was to be trying to buy drugs in Nevada, a state that had very tough drug laws at that particular time. He was worried that Jan would unknowingly try to buy cocaine from one of the many undercover narcotics officers patrolling the casinos. If Jan got busted, not only would it not go well for him, but Harrah's would have to cut us loose and that would be a shame.

We also had a bunch of Disneyland dates set up plus a very exciting Spring Break Budweiser concert in Daytona Beach for the spring. But if Jan got busted, we could probably kiss them all good-bye. This was not good news, not good news at all. My other business was now long gone, it would take me years to bring it back up to speed. Why would a guy that had absolutely nothing else going on in his life until now jeopardize all of this to suck some expensive white powder up his nose? Well that shows you how naïve I was.

I had to do something to fix this, but what? I had an idea. I asked the boss if he would be willing to help me help Jan. He said no problem.

"Okay here's what we can do," I said. "In about a half an hour, two or three of your plainclothes security guys will barge into our dressing room and pretend to be doing a drug bust on Jan. They have to have badges and handcuffs and be armed so they will look like real narcotics officers. Jan will never know the difference, so here's the scenario. Your guys will come into our dressing room and bust him, put the cuffs on him, and read him his rights being as tough as they can muster up. Then at the last moment you walk in and talk them out of locking him up, if he promises not to do drugs anymore." Where in the world did I come up with this stupidly naïve plan? Anyone with half a brain would have laughed me out of the room, but our boss was willing to give it a try, bless his heart.

Bam, the door flies open, four muscular men in suits come storming into our dressing room and order everybody out. Jan starts to stand up but they say not you buddy, you stay put. I could hardly contain myself. It was all I could do to keep from cracking up. I bolted out of the room and ran down the hallway to find a place to laugh out loud. I was in tears—what a performance. Jan looked scared shitless.

After a few minutes I went back towards the dressing room. Most of the band members were standing with their ears pressed up against the door. I joined them. It was really hard to hear much, but it was fun trying. After about thirty minutes or so the door opened up and the rent-a-cops filed out with their game faces still on and we were allowed back in. What a fuckin' sight, Jan sitting on the couch right where we left him and our boss was sitting next to him. Jan had his head on the bosses shoulder and was sobbing. All right, it seemed to have worked, hallelujah!

The two shows that night were great. Jan was giddy, and we were so proud of what we had pulled off. Our intervention had been brilliant, and Jan was well on his road to recovery by now, another hallelujah! Later that evening, maybe three or four hours after our last show, one of our guitar players, Mark Ward, who had hung around the casino to have drinks with some friends, went back to our dressing room to get his jacket. He unlocked the door and walked in. Huddled on the floor of the dressing room were Jan and three girls from the dancing troupe all snorting a pile of cocaine off of our dressing room mirror. Well, back to the drawing board.

I had just gotten my first, close-up introduction to the power of addiction. My parents didn't smoke or drink, I never saw stuff like that in my girlfriend's neighborhood in Malibu, and I never saw any of my typesetters, colors separators, or photostat technicians sitting around snorting cocaine. Yes, a few of my musician friends smoked a little weed from time to time, but I had never seen any of them do any hard drugs. Did I make the wrong choice for money? Did I really screw up a perfectly stable and comfortable life for this? Oh God, what am I going to do now?

All I could hope for was that Jan didn't get busted, at least until we completed our 1980 tour. Then I would reevaluate my options. It was too late to undo anything now. Over the next few months I tried everything trying to find the right combination of good cop, bad cop, and therapist, but the reality is that a drug addict only really cares about drugs. To complicate the problem even further, I was trying to talk logic to a once brilliant guy, who now had an IQ of 68. Now add drugs to 68 and that equals ...

But I had to make it work, I had no choice, I had committed to this. I had five band members, two roadies, two agents, a management partner, and a road manager all counting on having income for the next five to six months. I continued to keep a dialogue going with Jan, no matter how abstract and bizarre the dialogue was. One of the reoccurring themes was he didn't like Papa Doo Run Run. He accused them of sabotaging the songs he sang lead vocals on, which happen to be most of all of the Jan & Dean songs. He was convinced they were purposely mediocre on all of the Jan & Dean songs and then played brilliantly on The Beach Boys songs. Even the soundman, Richie, was in on the conspiracy. Jan was convinced the soundman was turning down the volume on his vocals. Could paranoia perhaps be linked to the use of cocaine ... ? Hmm. I told him I would look into all of this and get to the bottom of it, which seemed to make him happy at least for the moment.

The truth to all of this was, the reason the Jan & Dean songs that he sang the lead on had some sour notes was because he was the one singing those sour notes. This is not to say that the rest of us didn't hit our share of sour notes—of course we did, but he by far hit the most, night after night. But the reality is, the Jan & Dean songs are a lot more complicated than most of the other songs we were doing in our set. The irony here is that Jan wrote the musical arrangements for these songs when he had an IQ of 170. He went out of his way to make them as musically complex as creatively possible, and now they were too complicated for him to perform perfectly some sixteen years later with the brain damage he had suffered. The fact is, no one expects a live show to be perfect anyway, and fans were just happy to see Jan on stage performing the songs he so brilliantly produced back in the day. Our audiences were very forgiving, God bless them one and all.

Meanwhile, I had a new problem looming on the horizon. Papa Doo Run Run were not adjusting well to the loss of control they had over the money. As Papa Doo Run Run, they were used to doing the money collection, the bookkeeping, and cutting the checks to everyone themselves. But now, as a backup band for Jan & Dean, the guys that actually made those hits that they had been playing as a tribute band, things worked differently. I took that responsibility away from them and gave it to a real accounting firm who did accounting for Chicago, Steve Martin, and many others. Papa Doo Run Run could not understand why the bass player in the backup band shouldn't control the money.

I started to realize that the main problem we had was that Papa Doo Run Run didn't think of themselves as a backup band. In their minds, they had somehow assumed our identities. I tried to reason with them, but I wasn't getting anywhere. I now had two battlefronts going on at the same time. Working on a graphics project with Johnny Rivers or Linda Ronstadt now seemed like a walk in the park. How things change! Oh, and Papa Doo Run Run wanted to renegotiate their percentage deal. The fact that they had a percentage at all is astounding. How many backup bands get a percentage? I was way too generous, silly me, and I had created the monster. Almost all of my associates had told me not to do it, and now I was paying the price. I just needed to string this thing along to get through the last concert on the books. I told our agents not to book any more dates until I had a chance to reorganize. Then I would be ready for the 1981 season.

Toward the end of the 1980 summer tour, members of Papa Doo Run Run were becoming more defiant. I got the impression, however, that the two youngest guys, the two guitar players, weren't happy with the confrontation. One day I got another one of those brilliant ideas—divide and conquer. I got the two guitar players to meet with me without the other three guys, and I flat out told them that Papa Doo Run Run was a backup band, nothing more nothing less. They were really good, but they were expendable. I was tired of arguing with them, nothing was negotiable, the tail is never going to wag the dog, end of story. My instincts were right. The two of them were very happy with our current situation and confused by the position the two founding band members had taken.

I outlined my intentions, which were to do anything to get through the remaining ten to fifteen concerts, then take at least two months off toward the end of the year to reorganize. We would then audition for new band members, change anything that needed to be changed, and move on. I asked them if they wanted to be on the new team. They said yes. I also told them that being on the new team, I would need them to become moles in their own group. I needed to know what the other guys were thinking and planning. I didn't want to be caught off guard. I needed to know if there was a mutiny planned, or even if they were faking something, how far they would go. Having moles, I would know what the other side was thinking and could plan accordingly.

We shook hands, reiterating what a shame it was that it had come to this. None of us wanted to be deceitful, but there was no other way. If I told Papa Doo Run Run nothing was going to change, I had the feeling they might just up and bolt, leaving Jan and me stranded on the road with no band. I couldn't take that chance. A lot of buyers would also be stuck without a contracted band for their upcoming events.

So operation "string along" was now in effect. I tried not to lie; I tried to just be vague and not agree or disagree to anything. I was able to keep operation "string along" in place until the very last concert that was on the books, which was in Northern California, close to their home base. The militant Papa Doo Run Run guys were realizing that this was the last concert for a while, and they came to the realization that this could be their last stand. There would be no more leverage after this concert. I was informed that if they didn't have a certain signed document before they went on, they would not play for us. I asked the moles if the militants were serious. They said that two of them were—the bass player and the keyboard player—but in their opinion if push came to shove the drummer, Jim Shippey, would back us. So it appeared I had three out of five.

I suggested that in a worst-case scenario I could play guitar and one of the mole guitar players, who was also a very good bass player, could play bass. So we could get by with two guitars, bass, and drums. It would not be great, by any means, but the show would go on. The buyer would be happy, the audience would be happy to see Jan & Dean, and they probably wouldn't even notice that a keyboard and a bass player were missing. This could work.

The dressing room was tense. Jan had no idea what was going on except he had been told over the last couple of months that Papa Doo Run Run was on their way out—a prospect that made him very happy. We had about an hour to go before the show was to start and nothing had changed. We were still in a standoff. I thought I might try one more approach, because I really didn't want the mole band members to have to show their hands too soon. They had Papa Doo Run Run dates to do over the next few months, and they needed the income. I would be very busy reorganizing, so they could continue working until I was ready to roll out the new band. They would give Papa Doo Run Run at least thirty days' notice of their departure.

So I approached the band and informed them that no document was forthcoming. If they decided not to play, then I would be forced to walk out on stage with Jan to a packed audience in Northern California, their own backyard, and explain to the audience that our backup band, for reasons of their own, would not back us up on this afternoon, but that Jan and I would promise to come back in the very near future and play for them. End of dialogue.

They looked stunned. They went off by themselves to confer, and when they returned, they said they would play, but they wanted a meeting at my new Beverly Hills office on the following Monday morning to outline their demands and introduce some new ones. I agreed to meet with them. The concert came off without a hitch, our producer Bill Hollingshead was happy—it was fuckin' great.

The following Monday they all showed up at my new office complex, which actually had a conference room. Of course the moles had already filled me in on their demands. We all sat down. They had typed out their old and new demands. They handed me the documents, and I handed them right back with five envelopes. They wanted to know what the envelopes were.

"Those are your final payments," I said. They were shocked. I told them the documents weren't necessary and they were free to go pursue their other options. "Thank you for the year and a half, for the good times, of which there were many, and now this meeting is adjourned. Good luck gentlemen. I'll walk you to the door."

Over the next couple of months, we were involved in the process of assembling a new band. To try to appease Jan, I formulated a selection process that seemed to please everyone. The Moles, Jim and Mark, had one vote between them, Jan had one vote, and I had one vote—three votes total, majority won.

We had open auditions. The first guy selected was a former Beach Boys keyboard player, Gary Griffin (who is still with me thirty-five years later). Next, we narrowed down our choice of a bass player to two guys. One was a neighbor of mine, and the other was a guy from Michigan who had heard about our audition through the musicians union. He had never heard of Jan & Dean, but he was a quick learner and he needed a job. Both guys were talented bass players, but the young guy from Michigan could sing his ass off. His name was Chris Farmer, and he won the bass players play-off (and he, too, is still with me thirty-five years later).

The drummer was the next position to fill. And just to set the story straight, the drummer in Papa Doo Run Run, Jim Shippey, was a great guy who was not a problem at all, and would have probably jumped ship if we had asked him to—but Jan didn't like his playing, and for some reason Jan's main focus was on finding a drummer. I felt very lucky to have my four choices in place, so I had to let Jan have his pick. We ended up with Jan's first choice, a really fine drummer, but a guy who was a studio musician, not a road-tested, live concert musician. I figured it was no big deal. We had a band. And of course I was hoping that this would finally make Jan happy enough to stop using drugs. Brilliant, right?

15
APOCALYPSE NOW
SUMMER TOUR

{1981}

ow that we had a band again, our booking agent got really busy booking the 1981 summer tour. But it was decided that we should do some shakedown concerts first just to road test our new band. And we got the perfect offer—two weeks back at Harrah's Tahoe right into two weeks at Harrah's Reno. Four consecutive weeks with two shows a night was like doing a paid rehearsal. We would certainly know after this one-month run if we needed any more major changes or just some fine-tuning.

We flew into Tahoe, rented some cars, and drove to the condominiums we had rented for two weeks. Upon arriving at the condos the new drummer informs me that he was led to believe that everybody was getting their own condominium. I thought I had made it perfectly clear from the very beginning that we were a "recession" band and that everybody was expected to double up. In Tahoe each condo had three bedrooms, so everybody would certainly have their own room. The new drummer said he still needed to have a place to chant, or something like that, so I suggested he could walk about fifty yards and he would be in the woods where he could chant to his heart's delight. I had a feeling he didn't like that idea.

We were scheduled for a sound check at 5 p.m. that afternoon. At 4:30 p.m. everybody rallied to head for the sound check—except our new drummer. When we went to his condo to get him we found him leisurely cooking himself a steak. He said nobody told him when the sound check was. We told him we had to leave now, but he said he wanted to finish his steak, so we told him to get a taxi when he was through with dinner and we left. After an hour at the sound check without a drummer, we sent somebody back to the condo to look for him. He was sitting watching TV, and when asked why he hadn't taken a taxi he said the phone didn't work.

Arriving at the sound check he walks straight up to Jan and tells him that he was led to believe that we were sending some-one back to the condominium to get him. Jan says, more or less, oh don't worry about it because you are the best drummer in the world. Now I understood. He was Jan's boy and he could do what-ever he pleased. It was our first day and things were already going sideways. That night, I got together with the four other band mem-bers. We already realized that the new drummer needed to go. We had almost three weeks off when we got home, so we would have plenty of time to rehearse a new drummer, but we really had to start the search now. One of the guys said that John Cowsill of The Cowsills group was a drummer and a singer and that he was look-ing for work. I said call him tomorrow.

It never got any better. The four weeks seemed like four months. Jan wanted the band members' microphones way behind ours on stage. He complained that the band members talked too much, way more than they should, and that my guitar playing was really throwing him off and that I should stop playing so loud (I was unplugged). He also decided he needed a microphone with a radio in it just like John Denver's (since he had only one hand, he dropped microphones a lot) and he wants to sing "Hide Your Love Away" (a Beatles' song) because it's a song that is the best ever. Actually it's the only song beside Jan & Dean songs he could remember. That was just a little of what was going on onstage. Off the stage he was going to the blackjack tables. He was very frustrated because he was losing a lot of money. I tried to explain to him that hitting on eighteen is a bad idea and splitting two face cards was also a very bad idea. What the hell did I get myself into? Somehow we got through those four weeks.

Back in LA, John had started rehearsals with the band. He knew our songs pretty well, and he also knew The Beach Boys songs that we did. The big plus was that he was also a great vocalist. None of our other drummers sang. Having one more voice was very exciting. Our plan was to tell Jan that our last drummer quit. Jan didn't even know the guy's last name, and the guy had no way of reaching Jan.

One of the concerts I was looking forward to the most was a Spring Break concert for Budweiser Beer in Daytona Beach, Florida. This was free to the public, mostly college students, at the world famous Daytona Beach Bandshell, right on the beach at 2 p.m. on a Saturday. We arrived a week early, and spring break was in full bloom. Tens of thousands of young people were at the beach all day and then at the bars all night. The beer was flowing, the weather was perfect, and the vibe was right. We promoted the free concert all week long with the help of the Budweiser young adults marketing team plus an independent marketing team out of Westport, Connecticut.

The local wholesaler, Miss Helene, was worried that this concert was going to stiff big time. She informed me that last spring break, Miller Beer, their biggest competitor, tried putting on a concert at the Bandshell with Molly Hatchet, and "she" only drew three hundred people. Miller Beer had been very embarrassed about that, and she was really afraid that we (and her) were also going to fail to draw a crowd. Then Miller Beer would be having the last laugh. Corporate knew she was worried so they sent a young female executive, Miss Susan Vogelberger from the marketing department in St. Louis to Daytona Beach to calm down the wholesaler. This was the same Susan Vogelberger who walked by the amphitheater of our sold-out shows at Carowinds Park in North Carolina and had no idea who those performers Jan & Dean were. What a small world.

Meanwhile we were working every promotional trick in the book. And it really felt like it was working. The buzz (no pun intended) was everywhere. One of our favorite things to do was go to as many crowded bars as we could in one night carrying thousands of stickers promoting the concert. We would spread out on the crowded dance floor and sticker as many girls' butts as we could without getting caught. What a way to make a living!

Well, the big day came, and the police showed up at our hotel to get us through the traffic to the Bandshell. That seemed to be a good sign. *I'll bet that chick Molly Hatchet didn't have that problem.* The traffic was jammed for at least a half mile heading to the Bandshell and crowds on the beach were also heading in that direction. The police were already estimating the crowd to be at least twenty thousand plus, and it was still growing. We were almost two hours from the downbeat.

By the time we started playing, it looked like the crowd had doubled in size. Obviously this was a major grand-slam. The crowd sang and danced and batted around hundreds of free Budweiser beach balls. It was awesome. For the encore I pulled out all of the people from Budweiser Corporate and all the people from the wholesaler company including Miss Helene, the CEO, to come on stage to sing "Barbara Ann" with us. I told the crowd to thank these people for the awesome free concert, and they did, big time!

That night, we had our victory party at a very cool bar at a fancy hotel. The mood was over the top—this had been one of the biggest beach concerts ever. The Budweiser Corporate folks were over the moon. We all had put a ton of work into promoting this event and it had paid off big time. The president of the independent marketing company, George Blystone, came over to me during this loud and joyful celebration and introduced me to Miss Susan Vogelberger from corporate. She had a hibiscus in her hair. I was immediately hooked.

It was noisy so Susan and I slipped out and went across the street to a mini-mall. We found some chaise lounge chairs that were for sale, and I asked if we could try them out. They said okay. Somewhere in the conversation she told me, in the spirit of full disclosure, that when her boss said they were hiring Jan & Dean to headline the free beach concert at the Daytona Bandshell, she had said who? Her boss had then rattled off some of our songs, and she still had no clue. So he brought out his favorite Jan & Dean album cover and handed it to her. She still was clueless but she did point at the cover and say he's cute. Now she felt she needed me to know that she had pointed at Jan. I forgave her. We didn't buy the chairs, but we hung out for a couple of days until we both had to go back to work.

The 1981 tour was now named "The Apocalypse Now Summer Tour." I'm guessing you can figure out how it was going. Jan's drug use was getting progressively worse, and he was very unstable, both emotionally and mentally. By July, I knew it was over. But I really wanted to do the four Budweiser Spring Break concerts scheduled for March 1982. There was no way I could do those multiple dates with Jan, so I had to figure out how to hold on to them without including him. Somewhere in my memory banks, I recalled a conversation that I once had with my old friend Mike Love of The Beach Boys. He was lamenting the fact that the other Beach Boys wouldn't do corporate sponsored dates. They thought that it was "selling out." So I thought, why not call Mike and see if he would be interested in playing four spring break concerts with me on some of the most famous beaches in America. He loved the idea and there was even a bonus. RadioShack had shown a lot of interest in doing a deal with him, but the other Beach Boys weren't interested. So I said I would run it by Budweiser, and he said he would run the Mike and Dean collaboration by RadioShack. Within a few days we had both a Budweiser deal and a RadioShack deal.

I called for a meeting with my bandmates around a hotel pool in El Paso. We all couldn't wait for this tour to be over in late September. There were two and a half months left. But now I at least had some good news. I told them about the future Mike and Dean dates and they were thrilled; I had really made their day. Just having that to look forward to made the next two and a half months so much easier to endure.

I should mention here that at that time I was now courting Susan Vogelberger, who was still heavily involved in young adult marketing for the Budweiser brand in St. Louis. So I was now part of the Budweiser family.

So back to the tour. And okay, one more Jan story from the '81 Apocalypse Now Summer Tour. We were in New York playing some big outdoor event that we were headlining, so it was a big deal. I was told that Juice Newton might show up just to say hello, since she was a fan. She had a huge hit on the charts at the time, "Angel of the Morning," and that just happened to be one of Jan's favorite songs. Well she didn't show up until we had already gone on. But when we came off stage someone introduced her to me. We were going back on stage for the encore, so I invited her to come out on stage with us and sing "Barbara Ann" and she did. I introduced her and put her right in between Jan and me. The audience loved it. When we got off stage she said thank you very much, that was fun, gave me a hug, and off she went.

The next day we had off and Jan was already in a bad mood. He was always happiest onstage, so days off were not pleasant for him. My road manager came to my room and handed me some pictures that a fan had shot of the concert the day before that she had made some copies of. I loved the ones she took of us with Juice Newton. I thought, man, these will cheer Jan up for sure. So I headed for his room. I handed him the photos and said, "Check out these great pictures of us with Juice Newton." He stares at the pictures and then looks at me and says, "Where was I?"

"You were right there," I said, pointing at him right next to Juice. "That's you right there." Now he is really getting frustrated.

He asks again, "But where was I?"

And just think, I could have been back at my design studio, just finishing up someone's graphics project, getting ready to meet Harry Nilsson and Keith Moon at some famous Italian restaurant, where we would drink the night away, all the while pontificating on why everybody needs a "Point," or pointing out that a Point in every direction is like no Point at all. . . . And, where was I?

The "Apocalypse Now Summer Tour" had a new subtitle of "Beat the Clock Summer Tour." Over the next seven weeks we played in Ocean City, Maryland, Long Beach, California, with The Beach Boys, Tulsa, Kansas City, Hampton Beach, Meadowlands Stadium, Tonawanda, Long Island, Valley Forge Fair, Knoxville, Cincinnati, Indianapolis, Chicago, Columbia, Warwick, Westbury, Westport, Rochester, Seattle, Yakima, Portland, San Francisco, Santa Clara County Fair, Sacramento, Bakersfield, Magic Mountain, Phoenix, Denver, Duquesne, Louisville, Ft. Knox, Ft. Campbell, Ft. Bragg, Ft. Benning, Barksdale Airforce Base, FT. Hood, Ft. Sill, Tampa, and Atlanta.

The last concert of the tour was at a very cool rock-and-roll club called My Father's Place in Long Island, New York. Our friends The Turtles, Mark and Howard, dropped in and sang a few songs with us. It was so much fun! No huge drama from Jan, except that he wanted to get paid in cash before he went on because there was a film crew filming this last show and he needed to get extra money for the filming. We gave him the cash and the show went on and, miraculously, ended in two standing ovations. Turn off the lights, the party's over!

16

MIKE AND DEAN: THIS BUD'S FOR YOU

{1982–1983}

etting that ungrateful, unhappy, drug addicted human being out of my life was right up there with my first bicycle, my first kiss, my first hearing of "Why Do Fools Fall in Love" by Frankie Lymon and The Teenagers, my first car, my first sexual experience, my first wave, my first Dick Clark show, my first and only marriage and honeymoon, my first and second babies.

I hated Jan with a passion, not particularly because of how he treated me, but for what he did to himself. This was a once in a lifetime opportunity. To be able to relive a part of your life that was so incredible—I mean talk about being blessed. Most people when they lose something say, damn I thought it would never end, and if I had only known how quickly it could disappear, I would have done things a lot differently. And here we were given this grand opportunity to play rock and roll for appreciative fans all over—and Jan blows it because cocaine was more important than this once in a lifetime second chance. And he was the guy who had the most to lose. It was such a shame.

I couldn't have been happier. Such a weight was lifted off of me, and at the same time I was totally energized by all the exciting positive opportunities starting to take shape. I was in love, I had held on to the Budweiser Spring Break project, and I was working with really talented people that I respected, admired, and truly liked. We were no longer burdened by Jan's limitations and unpredictability.

Mike Love also seemed reenergized. He had experienced many of the same problems I had, plus some. Brian Wilson, a brilliant composer and record producer, was a mental case, and Dennis Wilson was an unpredictable drunk with an uncontrollable mean streak and a really bad temper—especially when he was around Mike. Each individual guy had his own advisor or manager or guru and attorney. How in the world was it possible to make any decisions and get anything done? It was a nightmare for Mike. But when we got together, it only took us a few minutes to make decisions—then we'd go to lunch. If you're drug and alcohol free, happy to be doing what you're doing, giving thanks to God every day that you can still make a living playing and singing rock and roll, what's there to be pissed off at? I just didn't get it.

Working with Anheuser-Busch was a godsend. Not only did I meet the girl I fell in love with and married, but I finally got to work with a real company, doing the things a real company does. Anheuser-Busch made record companies look like a combination of a snake oil salesman convention and a street corner hot dog stand. The business theory used at these different businesses were polar opposites. After working with the folks at Budweiser, I wondered how the hell record companies stayed in business. They had to be selling drugs. And if they were, it probably wasn't a bad idea, since most of their consumers would be in-house anyway. That would alleviate any cumbersome distribution problems for sure. Nowadays it's pretty evident how record companies stay afloat— they are owned by real companies like Time Warner, Sony, GE, Disney, RCA, ABC, NBC, and EMI.

Anheuser-Busch knew that money bought money, if spent in the right places. They wanted me to help design the Mike and Dean

Spring Break marketing program. This included the event poster, t-shirts, beach towels, beer holders and beer mugs, Frisbees, backstage passes, and even our own Budweiser tour jackets. And they paid me to do this even when I told them I'd do it for free. They also loved the idea of Mike and Dean recording a custom song for Budweiser to be pressed up on a vinyl 45 on the Budweiser label to be given away for promotion.

Starting two months before spring break they had me doing five to ten phone interviews a day from my home in California, and at a month out from spring break they would pay me to do a promotional tour promoting our own free concerts on the beach. As I remember, I made more money promoting the Mike and Dean concerts then I made playing the concerts. But the truth is, I spent a lot more time promoting the concerts than the two hours on stage at each of the four different concert sites.

Meanwhile it had been two to three months since I had last talked to Jan. I had received a telegram from him telling me to cease and desist all Jan & Dean business, and then a month later, after the telegram, he left me a message that it was time for me to come up to his dad's house and rehearse with the new band. Yeah, sure, I'll be right over. What did he do, take a page from the Papa Doo Run Run "Art of Negotiating" handbook? I had no desire to talk to him, his dad, his drug dealer, his band—screw them all. I was busy and loving every minute of it. Now Jan started calling every day or so and leaving messages about how good the new band is and that I needed to relearn all of my vocal parts with the new band because unlike the band that I (and he) hired, his new band knew all the right chords, baby.

I couldn't fucking believe it. He wasn't getting the message that I had fired him, not the other way around. He was so delusional that he thought he had fired me and I must be waiting by my phone, wringing my hands waiting for him to rehire me. It was also very evident that the band was equally ignorant. They were going to his house every day now for going on two months. They must be really busy guys. Evidently they had been listening to this doped-up guy for months. Any real musician would know in a New York minute that he was not all there. The wheel is turning but the hamster is dead. I couldn't fathom how they hadn't figured out that rehearsing with this guy was a total waste of time. What could Jan be telling them to make them stick around? I just knew Jan and his dad were not paying them to rehearse. I was sure of that. I was actually starting to feel sorry for them.

Jan's behavior, besides the drugs, came from him needing to control constantly. He was a control freak. That's why he hated Papa Doo Run Run. They had their own business; they didn't really need him. And our 1981 band were all individually talented musicians. If they weren't playing with Jan & Dean, they would be playing for someone else. They didn't need him (or me) and that drove him crazy. What Jan was looking for were individuals who had even less going for themselves than he did, and this way he could control them. If they didn't have any other options, they would be desperate enough to keep hanging in there waiting for that future check.

By now I was having to fly to corporate Anheuser-Busch in St. Louis and then on to Westport, Connecticut, where the independent marketing company was based, then back to Anheuser-Busch where I stayed at Susan's house. I would call home to get my messages, and Jan was now calling me multiple times a day. He was no longer sounding so arrogant. He had started to plead for me to come rehearse, saying that the band was really looking forward to meeting me. I'll bet they were.

One day I am sitting in Susan's office using her typewriter when the phone rings and her secretary tells her Jan is calling and he is looking for me. Oh shit, he still knows how to ruin a beautiful day. I pick up the phone.

"Yes Jan, what do you want?" He says he knows that I am about to work with Mike Love, and he doesn't want me to do it. Then he says that he will sue me if I do. Oh boy, he has me shaking in my Adidas. Then he started swearing at me so I hung up the phone. He called back. I told him to send me a telegram like the last one he sent me and hung up again. The phone rings again and we let it keep ringing. A couple of days later he reaches us again. Now he is pleading with me not to work with Mike. I asked why. He says that it hurts him. Now let me get this straight. He thinks he has fired me, then takes over our business, so I get a new job and it hurts him? I guess he had expected to find me back at my old gas station job, standing under a lube rack, changing the oil on an old beige Plymouth. I told him to stop calling me and hung up.

The next day I hit the road. I was heading to the marketing company's home base in Westport, Connecticut. A few days later, George Blystone and I would go cross-country to Lake Tahoe and link up with Mike Love to take some pictures for our spring break concert promo package. The Beach Boys were playing Caesar's Tahoe for three nights and Mike asked me if I wanted to join them on stage that night. When I showed up on stage I noticed a few guys were missing. Carl Wilson was off working on a solo music project, Dennis Wilson had gotten pissed off at something and gone back to Los Angeles, and Brian Wilson was back to not touring with the band. So Mike, Alan, and Bruce Johnston were The Beach Boys.

I was asked to do a little more than my usual guest routine as a result. Jan & Dean had a solid, hard-core fan base in Tahoe, and there had always been a big Beach Boys and Jan & Dean fan base overlap, which both groups had always nurtured. So when I joined them on stage, I got a great response, and we all had a great evening playing together. It was very special. I was invited to play through the end of their engagement, and I really, really wanted to. I had often fantasized about being a part-time or maybe even a permanent member of The Beach Boys. We had always had great chemistry together and the historical threads that kept us bound were long and intricate. Plus I didn't bring any negative baggage—no drugs, no arrests, no therapists, no ex-wives, no lawsuits, no draft dodging, no bankruptcies. Jesus, I sound pretty freaking boring.

Unfortunately I couldn't stay. George and I had an important dinner meeting in St. Louis with the head of the young adult marketing team at Budweiser the following day. I agonized over my situation. I was bouncing back and forth between going and staying. In the rock-and-roll world I could stay and reschedule the dinner meeting, but now that I was in the corporate world, I knew I had to go to St. Louis. Besides the meeting, I had to deliver the many rolls of film we had just taken in Tahoe to be processed and prepared for the campaign.

Once all the graphic production stuff was in the works, I devoted all of my time to doing interviews from home, over the phone mostly, with print media, talk radio, and oldies stations. Actually I really enjoy doing interviews. I considered it an honor that people cared enough to ask me a question about anything, and I always felt very flattered.

When the concerts were a little more than a month away, the promotional tour was all set up and ready to go, and it was time for me to hit the road again. About a day before I was going to leave, I got a call from Tom Hewlette, The Beach Boys' manager who had just merged with Jerry Weintraub, a movie producer. He summoned me to his posh Beverly Hills office. I was trying to figure out why he wanted to talk to me. It was a total mystery. I showed up mainly out of respect but also curiosity. After some small talk, Tom got finally got to the point. My association with Mike Love and the Budweiser project were causing some internal and some external problem within The Beach Boys organization, so he was asking me to please abandon the Mike and Dean project.

I was stunned and confused. I looked around for Big Guido or Sammy the Bull standing with bulges under their shiny suit jackets, but there was nobody, just Tom and me. I was trying to figure out why in the world he would be asking me to do this without some kind of leverage—like the threat of being whacked if I didn't. I guess I needed to ask him a question, and the first question was a beaut.

"Tom, shouldn't you be talking to Mike Love? You are his manager, aren't you. Why don't you ask Mike to abandon the project?" Actually it was pretty clear to me that either he had already talked to Mike and Mike blew him off, or he was afraid to talk to Mike. You know something, I don't even remember what he said. He kind of danced around the question—and probably for good reason.

"Okay Tom, let's put the commitment part aside for now, but why would I walk away from this project? Why would I walk away from this grand opportunity to move on from Jan & Dean, and why would I walk away from the income?" Tom blew right by the commitment part and got right to it.

"Okay how much income are we talking about?" he asked.

"Plenty when it's all added up," I said. "Graphics money, promotion money, and performance money."

"What if I add you into The Beach Boys until you make the equivalent amount you would lose, plus a bonus, how about that?" Tom said. Now if he had said I would be a Beach Boy for a year or two or three, and I got a piece of Brian Wilson's publishing income, and my pick of any of Dennis Wilson's girlfriends or cars or boats, I might have thought that one over. But to just make about the same amount of money, and let my friends at Anheuser-Busch down, there was no way. He better call Guido.

"No, Tom, I can't do that. We are five weeks out. I am committed heart and soul to this project. If you can talk Mike into pulling out I suppose that's his business." The fact that Tom was even talking to me spoke volumes about what Mike's mindset was about all of this. I walked out of that meeting shaking my head at how weird that meeting had been. Oh no, was Guido waiting by my car with an offer I couldn't refuse? Well, I bet Guido is probably still looking for my black Porsche in valet parking. He obviously doesn't know me very well. I never pay for valet parking. I had parked on the residential side street and walked three blocks to Tom's office.

I had to fly back to St. Louis to meet with the promotion team and the public relations people before I headed out on the Mike and Dean promotional tour. Once again Jan reaches me at Susan's office. He is very upset. His new band members, who were now just completing three months of rehearsals, are now demanding to be paid for all their rehearsals. Jan's dad won't pay them, so they up and quit. Jan was crying. He wanted to join Mike and me. I asked him if he had gotten some drug intervention of any sort. He said he didn't need any help, he didn't have a drug problem, he was only doing a gram a day and that was because of me—I caused it all. I told him that Mike and I were working for Anheuser-Busch, a very successful and conservative company. We couldn't allow someone with a drug addiction to perform with us.

"But now I will tell you what to do," I said, "and if you do it, that's when we will talk about any possible future together. So here it is. You enroll in the CA program for addiction, stay in it and clean for a year, and then we will go from there. I suggest you start tomorrow, since you don't have to rehearse anymore. You can look forward to talking about your musical future one year from now. The sooner you start, the sooner the year will be up. Those are the conditions. If you want perform again, you will do it. If cocaine means more to you than performing, then so be it."

"That's bullshit," Jan said. So I hung up. A few minutes later the phone rings again.

"Let's go to dinner," I said to Susan. Well at least he isn't driving us to drugs, but he is driving us into overeating.

A few days later I headed out for Florida and then from there to Texas—both huge target markets. My typical promotion day went something like this. Mornings: drive time oldies radio; mid-mornings: talk radio shows and print media; noontime: radio or

TV; early afternoon: print media and a visit to the wholesaler's office; late afternoon: drive time radio. Then I'd take an hour and a half for a good dinner, more radio, then to the best bar accounts for some handshaking and beer guzzling, then back to the hotel to rest and to do it all over again the next day. What a blitz. It was working great. We were promoting four free beach concerts, and Budweiser was picking up the tab. At these beach concerts everybody got a free hat or visor, beach ball (while they lasted), Frisbee, and beach towel. Ain't America great!

In El Paso as I walked through the lobby of my hotel, I looked out the window and noticed the pool. It looked very familiar to me. Hey, this is the pool where we had that band meeting last summer and I told the guys that this was our last tour for a while. But I told them something else was in the works and to be patient. Seven months later and here I am, and they will be joining me and Mike in a couple of weeks. The dream came true.

The first big day finally arrived. It was a beach concert in South Padre Island, Texas. I met Mike when his helicopter arrived and we headed to the hotel. I passed out our custom-made Budweiser tour jackets to everybody, and then we headed to our beautiful stage right on the sand, on a great beach, and the weather was picture-perfect! The cops that had caravanned us to the concert site said the crowd estimate was as many as thirty thousand, the biggest crowd they had ever see on that beach. Walking on that stage for the first time was surreal. Our set list was to die for, the playing and the singing was effortless, the vibe was heavenly. I was so proud to have put this project together and to have it work out so well. And on top of everything else, it was so much fun fun fun. The whole team, from top to bottom, were the best and the brightest in the business. What a glorious day!

The next day we flew a charter flight to Daytona Beach where Jan & Dean had played the year before. In a few days we would do it all over again. The Daytona Beach spring break concert also went extremely well. Somewhere in there, I proposed to Susan, and to my surprise, she accepted. We got married the following June in beautiful downtown Baltimore and honeymooned in the Bahamas, staying at my business partner Winston Simone's beautiful home on the beach in Lyford Cay.

A few days after the Daytona Beach concert, we flew to Fort Lauderdale and did it again. Another home run! And another few days later we flew to Fort Walton and did our last Budweiser beach party—and yes, another homerun.

We were on a roll and Budweiser wanted to do more Mike and Dean dates. Mike had also had positive feedback from the Tandy Corporation (RadioShack), another successful, conservative company out of Texas. We ended up doing a bunch of concerts and other exciting recording projects for the Tandy Corporation. It was all working out even better than we had hoped. Mike and I were even interviewed on a beautiful sailing yacht by Robin Leach for *Lifestyles of the Rich and Famous,* so I guess that meant we were rich and famous, imagine that!

Over the next eight months, Mike and I did a lot more work for Budweiser and RadioShack; we even recorded some songs together at Mike's studio in Santa Barbara. Everything we did was fun and simple and our clients were so appreciative of the effort we put into each and every project.

Back home I was getting a lot of calls from Jan. He informed me that he joined Cocaine Anonymous and had been clean for three months. I congratulated him on his newfound sobriety, but reminded him that he needed to stay clean for a whole year before we could talk about any future plans. I think he was hoping that we could start those talks sooner, but I held my ground and made it clear that he needed to stay on that path of recovery until he completed one year of sobriety, and then we could talk about doing music together again. He said he would try his hardest to stay clean.

17

REUNITING?

{1983–2004}

F our or five months later, I'm at Susan's parents' house in Baltimore, and we had just celebrated Christmas 1983. I get a call from some media person asking me for my thoughts about the drowning death of Dennis Wilson. I was stunned to hear Dennis had died. I had cared a lot about Dennis. We were buddies, and we had always gotten along. When we were together he had always been fun-loving Dennis (although around Mike he was a totally different person). I was sad to hear how tragically he had died—alone and unhappy. On the other hand, I hoped he was finally at peace.

The passing of Dennis seemed to stabilize The Beach Boys. Mike now had better control, and his first responsibility was to help with the reorganization of his own group, which had a lot more potential than working with me. I completely agreed and even offered my services for whatever I could do to help the rebranding of The Beach Boys.

Now it became obvious that I needed a new day job. Well, back to the drawing board—literally—or hope that Jan would stay sober and maybe we could put the band back together, just like the Blues Brothers did. I dabbled in some graphic projects and finished a few recording projects with Mike. Meanwhile, Jan kept checking in. He was now eight months clean, and he did sound a lot better. Damn, could this possibly work out just as planned?

I started to get calls about the availability of Jan & Dean. There still seemed to be quite a bit of interest. One guy in particular, Bill Hollingshead, was really interested in resuming booking dates for us. We had done a bunch of very successful dates with him over the years, including that last Papa Doo Run Run concert. The bonus was that Jan liked and trusted him. Bill said he had a very big and important date coming up, and his client really wanted Jan & Dean. I was really confused about what to do but I wasn't really sure why. After I thought about it, I realized that deep down I didn't think Jan could stay sober. The odds were against it. I never dreamed I would actually consider reuniting with him again after the nightmare he put us through over those last two years.

I kept stalling Bill for an answer, and I was still expecting a drug-crazed call from Jan ordering me to come to his house and rehearse with his brand new band, The Coke Brothers aka The Columbian Bam Bam Band. But that never happened. So after another round of calls from people enquiring about the status of Jan & Dean, and more calls from "David Niven" (Jan's nickname when he was happy, charming, and agreeable), I made the decision. Even though it wasn't exactly a year of sobriety, it was close enough, and Bill Hollingshead really needed an answer ASAP. So I said yes to reuniting Jan & Dean at Bill's upcoming event.

But one more piece of business. I needed Jan and his dad to agree to my new set of demands.

1. I am in full control, period, and if you can't agree to that, then we have nothing further to talk about. But if you agree to that then here are the rest of my demands.

2. I am the only partner, Jan will be on a negotiated salary period. And in return, I will create a concert merchandising business that Jan can control and he may keep all the proceeds.

3. All I ask of Jan is to show up sober, physically, mentally, and emotionally, ready to perform.

They realized that they really had no leverage, so they agreed to my terms.

The Reunited Concert was held on May 3, 1983, in San Bernardino, California, at the sixty-eighth annual Orange Show. The band had rehearsed the song "Reunited" by Peaches and Herb, and as a surprise, they played it when Jan and I walked on stage together. The audience of over four thousand loved it and so did we.

Over the next twenty-one years, we got to play over fifteen hundred concerts, and what an awesome ride it was. We got to play some very special venues and traveled to some very interesting places. Some of the more memorable venues we have played include the likes of The Rose Bowl (four times), Three Rivers Stadium (three times), Murphy Stadium (three times), Mile High Stadium, The LA Forum, The Hollywood Bowl, The Greek Theatre (twice), The Universal Amphitheatre, The Honolulu International Center Arena, The Sports Arena, The Mill Run Theatre, Mall of the Americas, The Roxy, The Whiskey, Pandora's Box, The Plush Pup, The Itchy Foot Mose Beer Bar, The Beverly Hills Hotel, The Santa Monica Civic Auditorium, The Honolulu Band Shell, The Kona Hilton Hotel, Pearl Harbor Bloch Arena, The Bread Crumb Parking Lot, Knotts Berry Farm, Disneyland, Disneyworld, Magic Mountain, Santa Cruz Boardwalk (four times), The Orange County Fair (five times), The Pacific Amphitheatre, The Valair Ballroom, The Surf Ballroom, Noah's Waterpark (five times), Summerfest (four times), The Sands Casino, Harrah's Casino, Caesars Casino,

The Stardust Casino, The Island Casino, The Aladdin Casino, The Alaska State Fair, The California State Fair, The Ohio State Fair, The Tulsa State Fair, The New Mexico State Fair, The Montana State Fair, The New York State Fair, The Delano State Fair, The Washington State Fair, The Oregon State Fair, Hot August Nights (four times), Route 66 Rendezvous, Cruisin' the Coast, Andy's Picnic, Linda's Birthday Party, In-N-Out's 50th Birthday Party, Carroll Shelby's 80th Birthday Party, The Daytona Band Shell, California Adventure's New Year's Party, The Grand Ole Opry House, The Crazy Horse Saloon, The Palomino Club, The Delmar Beach Club, The Capitol Club, The Old Golden Bear and The New Golden Bear, The Jolly Lounge, The Ocean City Boardwalk, The Waterfront Hilton Grand Opening, The Huntington Beach Hyatt Resort Grand Opening, and we even played twelve bizarre concerts in the People's Republic of China. We even played six nights at The Shanghai Sports Arena, a twenty thousand seater and it was sold out all five nights.

The concert at the East County Center for the Performing Arts in El Cajon, California, March 6, 2004, unbeknownst to us at the time, ended up being the last Jan & Dean concert. Shows were becoming more and more difficult to pull off because of the many physical problems Jan had to overcome. But you know he always did pull it off, much to the delight of his many supportive and adoring fans. That night he received his usual three standing ovations and was helped off of the stage by the stage crew, straight into his dressing room, where he could cool down and catch his breath. Later that evening we helped him walk to his car, eased him into the passenger seat, helped him put his seatbelt on, then watched him drive off with his wife Gertie. That's the last time we saw him. Three weeks later he had a seizure followed by a heart attack and died at his beautiful home in Brentwood, California, at the age of sixty-three.

A few weeks later, our most beloved musical partner Lou Adler hosted an awesome memorial party at one of Jan's favorite places in the world besides Hawaii—The Roxy (I designed the neon logo) on the Sunset Strip. Many of our old high school buddies came, along with many old musical pals as well. As you can guess, the stage at The Roxy didn't go to waste. Jan's brother Kenny, who owns one of the largest studio instrument rental businesses in the world, SIR, filled the stage with instruments, and it turned into a full-blown jam session. We also used the stage to tell some of our favorite Jan stories, which were legendary. He would have loved it. His parents, Bill and Clara, had a big and beautiful booth were they chatted the night away with many of Jan's old high school friends who had spent many a day and many a night making some of their happiest teenage memories at the Berrys' house on Linda Flora Drive in Bel Air.

I have to say it was a great evening. It was also an awesome fifty-five years—we had a great run, and I am sure glad we met.

POSTSCRIPT

happened to watch the last part of the 2014 Glen Campbell documentary, "I'll be Me," when it was recently shown on CNN. The documentary follows Glen on his last concert tour. You get to see everything behind the scenes that went on day-to-day as he went from city to city to perform. You get to see how difficult it was hour by hour to get someone ready to do a show who is suffering from the onset of Alzheimer's Disease. I knew the story, but I had not seen the documentary when it first aired. I really had a visceral reaction to everything I was seeing. An obvious trigger was that Glen was a very dear friend, and nobody wants to see this happen to a loved one, but the other trigger was that this was exactly what I went through with Jan in at least the last two to three years that we were still performing. My performance day ritual with Jan was very similar to what the Campbell family went thru on their last concert tour. The mood swings, the confusion, and the paranoia were all present for the viewer to see. None of what I went through was captured on film, thank God, but it's still very vivid in my memory, so when I saw Glen's full range of emotions it was way too familiar to me.

I recalled a particularly rough travel day (one of many) when Jan and I, plus our band, flew into Louisville, Kentucky, early one morning. We had played the night before, so nobody had gotten much sleep. We were headlining the grandstand show at the Kentucky State Fair, and our soundcheck was midafternoon, so the band needed to get to that sound check on time. Our plane had gotten in around 7:30 a.m. Our plan was to go directly to the hotel, get Jan into his room where he could take a long nap until we left for the show at maybe 7:00 that evening, and we would hit the stage around 9:00. Our band could also get some nap time until they got picked up to go to the midafternoon sound check. Then they could come back to the hotel, grab a bite to eat, get dressed, and be ready to depart for the show when our ride showed up. That was our plan.

But getting off the airplane, Jan hits his arm on the airplanes main cabin door and he says he is in pain. I told him that the hotel was twenty minutes away, and we can get some Tylenol when we check in and he can go to bed. He said no, he wants to go to the hospital now. We head to baggage claim where we were picking up our bags and meeting our transportation. We got in the van and told the driver to take us to the hotel please. Jan says no, take me to the hospital. I told Jan that we needed to get the band to the hotel first, and then we could go to the hospital. He wasn't happy about that, but I told the driver to continue to the hotel. We get to the hotel, drop off the band, and the driver takes us to the hospital and parks by the emergency room entrance. Jan wants a wheelchair, so I get out of the van and look for one. I spot just one chair so I go grab it. Holy shit, its one of those old wood and wicker wheelchairs you see in some of those creepy old black and white movies. I hoped Jan wouldn't notice. I load him into the chair and tell the driver I'll call him when we are ready to go back to the hotel, and then I wheel Jan into the emergency waiting room.

Holy shit again—it's full of street people either bleeding or looking really sick. It's just past eight o'clock in the morning, so you can imagine what it looked and smelled like. I wheel Jan to a spot against the wall in between two tough looking guys who looked like they've had been in a fight or something. I take Jan's wallet to the receptionist and give her all of Jan's insurance information and she starts typing. I look around at the chaos in the room. There had to be thirty people waiting to see a doctor. This is a nightmare, and just think, we are supposed to be playing in about twelve hours. Luckily for me Jan is nodding off, so he is no longer asking why this is taking such a long time.

As I am viewing all of this, I see healthy looking doctors dressed in their clean hospital gear taking care of lots of patients. That was Jan's dream many years ago, and now I look over at him slouched over in that pathetic old wood and wicker wheelchair and wonder how all of this had happened. I needed to find some humor in all of this sensory overload. So I imagined gathering up some of those button-down doctors, asking them to come into the emergency waiting room, and then offering a thousand dollars to whomever could look around that room and pick out the person that will be headlining a music concert at the Grandstand Stage that night at the Kentucky State Fair. Hey, I would even give them maybe three guesses each. I was pretty damn sure that Jan would have been their very last choice.

Yes, we got out of there in about five hours and the show went on. It was another home run, and the next day we were off to the next one.

So back to Glen's documentary. Toward the end of the documentary, the Campbell Family realizes that shows are increasingly getting much harder to pull off as Glen's mental health declines. They are trying to find that balance between giving Glen a stage to say his long good-bye to his adoring fans and at the same time not crossing the line of embarrassing himself musically. He could really damage the legacy of the Glen Campbell brand if he continued to play much longer. The family, including a son and daughter who are in his band, make the hard decision that they will finish the last couple of dates on this current tour and that will be The End. And that's how the documentary also ends. I was happy for them that they really did do a great job under very difficult conditions, and that Glen was able to play music with his family all around him for that one last time. The blessing is that he is not sitting somewhere wishing he was still on stage and remembering everything that he has lost.

I realized that the Jan & Dean ending was a lot longer than it should have been and not very clean. I had intended to end it when Jan could no longer stand on stage through a whole concert. There were times when he sat back by the drum riser when we would do our dance medley, which was ten to fifteen minutes long at most, and then he would rejoin us for the rest of the show. But during our last two years of performing, he couldn't stand at all during a show. He wanted to sit in a chair in the middle of the stage the whole performance. I pleaded with him to try to exercise during the off-season so he could stand for most of a performance. I even told him that if he wasn't any longer able to stand on stage, we would have to retire Jan & Dean. I thought that this would motivate him to change his diet and try some sort of exercise program. His brother Kenny, offered to buy him a state of the art treadmill, just for walking. But his health was too diminished at this point, and it was too late to correct anything.

So now what do I do. I am damned if I do and damned if I don't. Jan's hard-core fans don't care if he sits, and they are going to resent me if I pull the plug. He will have nothing to look forward to, and he would probably hate me and die of a broken heart. And guess who will get the blame. On the other hand, if we keep going to keep him happy, he will most certainly damage the legacy of Jan & Dean and leave the fans with that sad memory of the last time they saw him, sitting on a chair in the middle of the stage. I announced in the summer of 2002, about two years before he passed away, that this would be our "Aloha Tour" (farewell), and I fully intended for that to be our last tour. We played at one of our favorite events that year, Hot August Nights, a hot rod festival in Reno, Nevada. We played that event at least six times, and it was always a blast! But now it was really sad knowing this was the last time Jan & Dean would ever play there.

From *The Reno Gazette-Journal*
September 11, 2002
Letters to the Editor

JAN & DEAN WERE INSPIRATIONAL

I'd like to thank Jan and Dean for their joyous farewell concert here in Reno. Special thanks to Jan for his courage and getting out there despite his tragic auto accident and the disabilities he received. I also have serious health problems and now my motto is, "Life is either too long or too short to not get out there and enjoy yourself," so when they invited dancers young and old, to join them on stage during their dance medley you can bet I was there "dancin' like no one was lookin'."

From the size and mood of the crowd I wondered if others felt as I do, especially after September 11, just a year ago. I want to get back to a simpler time and place and dance to Jan and Dean's music as my personal celebration of life. Thank you so much Jan and Dean for all the wonderful music and memories we all shared and will never forget!

Debbie, *Reno, Nevada*

Then by the end of the year I was hearing from so many fans like her who didn't want us to "hangem' up" until they saw us one more time. But I was also hearing rumblings from our booking agents and buyers saying that Jan had become a liability because buyers and venues were worried that he would fall and hurt himself on stage, and they would unfortunately be liable for a lawsuit, so they would have to pass on hiring us from this point on. We still had many solid offers in 2003—places I really wanted to play one more time, so should I extend the "Aloha Tour" one more year? I was very conflicted. I really needed to end it, but I still had Jan to worry about. I could keep going with my bandmates, plus The Beach Boys were asking me if I wanted to do some dates with them so I could keep playing. But Jan wouldn't be able to play without me, and he would probably retreat into his bedroom totally depressed and die.

I decided to extend the Farewell Tour for one more year and figured God will let me know when to end it or He will end it. A little over a year later Jan passed away, a few weeks after playing at a beautiful performing arts center where, despite sitting in a chair in the middle of the stage and not looking all that healthy, he got either two or three standing ovations, and he headed home from that concert looking forward to the next concert.

A few years later, while playing with basically my same group of guys, a fan approached me after a show and asked for an autograph. Then he asked me a very interesting question that maybe many of our fans were curious about but wouldn't have had the nerve to ask. He asked me why I continued touring with Jan when it was obvious he was not very healthy and was noticeably holding us back musically, based on what he had just seen. I told him simply that yes, I had two choices, one that would benefit the legacy of Jan & Dean and one that would benefit Jan, and I chose Jan, and it was the right thing to do at the time. Glad you enjoyed the concert.

ABOUT THE AUTHOR

Photo by Jillian Torrence

Rock legend Dean Ormsby Torrence is the cofounder and cowriter of songs for the hit duo Jan & Dean. Born in Los Angeles in 1940, Torrence helped pioneer the California Sound during the sixties with surf rock hits like "Surf City" and "Dead Man's Curve."

At the height of their career Jan & Dean had sixteen Top 40 hits, a total of twenty-six chart hits, and hosted and performed at the historic *T.A.M.I. Show*. They won six gold records, one Grammy plus numerous nominations, and appeared seventeen times on Dick Clark's American Bandstand.

Torrence cowrote the screenplay of Jan & Dean's story featured in the 1978 movie of the week, *Deadman's Curve.*

He also formed a successful graphic design studio after receiving a degree in advertising design from the school of Architecture and Fine Arts at the Univeristy of Southern California (USC). He is the designer of the logo for The American Music Awards as well as The Beach Boys logo and The Roxy logo.

Torrence lives in Huntington Beach, "Surf City," with his wife of thirty-four years and has two beautiful daughters, Katie, age 26, and Jillian, age 22. He continues to tour with his band, the Surf City Allstars.